*"It seems that the best investment you could make is in building a high fence between you and the Joneses. Angie Grainger's new book confronts us all with some reality and responsibility checks and puts the financial focus where it belongs- between our ears- and helps us all make money decisions that will pay off in the long run. Read it now if you want to get your own financial house in order."*
> **Mitch Anthony, Author, *The New RetireMentality, The Cash In The Hat, and The Bean Is Not Green,* Founder, The Financial Life Planning Institute**

*"In The Joneses Are Broke!, Angie brings a fresh innovative approach to looking at building wealth and finding true happiness. Driving the importance of setting goals, planning and taking action, Angie reinforces personal accountability and discipline for those ready to make real improvements in their financial lives. Right on point for this new economy."*
> **Gary Ryan Blair-TheGoalsGuy, *Author of Everything Counts!, Goal-Setting 101, The Ten Commandments of Goal Setting, and more.***

*"Angie Grainger's new book, The Joneses Are Broke!, is right on the money! Offering fresh insights and understanding about the state of our financial affairs, Angie helps readers to not only understand how and why they got where they are, but more importantly, how to change for the better. The Joneses Are Broke! provides real solutions that can easily be followed by anyone. I will be recommending this book as a "must read" to all of our clients."*

**Deborah Price, Author, *Money Magic: Unleashing Your True Potential for Prosperity and Fulfillment*, Founder & CEO, The Money Coaching Institute**

*"Fasten your seat belts and hang on because the most important journey of your life is about to begin, and you don't want to miss out! Whether you have achieved your life's ambitions or not, it is time for everyone to become liberated with Angie's 49 Secrets of MoneyTM. Her brilliantly penned tie in with "RETHINKing" your life through Learn, Act, and Remember, ties into the essence of what IS necessary in life to live it with passion and purpose. Take action today and experience a powerful impact on your life."*

**Leonard C. Wright, CPA/PFS, CFP, CLU, ChFC, Money Doctor, American Institute of Certified Public Accountants: http://www.360financialliteracy.org. Co-host - Financial Fridays AM 670 KMZQ, Las Vegas, Nevada**

# The Joneses Are
# BROKE!

## Stop trying to keep up with them…

## Liberate yourself with the 49 Secrets of Money!

**Angie Marie Grainger,
CPA/PFS, CFP®
Certified Money Coach**

Copyright © 2010 by Angie Marie Grainger

All rights reserved

No part of this book may be reproduced, stored in a retrieval system, or transmitted by any means, electronic, mechanical, photocopying, recording, or otherwise, without written permission from the publisher. No patent liability is assumed with respect to the use of the information contained herein. Although every precaution has been taken in the preparation of this book, the publisher and author assume no responsibility for errors or omissions. Neither is any liability assumed for damages resulting from the use of information contained herein.

Printed in the United States of America

First Printing: November 2010

Publisher's Cataloging-in-Publication Data

Grainger, Angie Marie.

> The Jones Are Broke!: Stop trying to keep up with them... liberate yourself with the 49 Secrets of Money.

Angie Marie Grainger.

> p. cm.

ISBN 978-0-615-42002-8

> 1. Finance, Personal. 2. Self Improvement/Self Help 3. Financial security. 4. Wealth. 5. Retirement income. 6. Wealth—Psychological aspects. I. Title

Logo design by Deseo Artistico

# TABLE OF CONTENTS

ACKNOWLEDGEMENTS ............................................. 1
INTRODUCTION .................................................. 3
CHAPTER 1: Meet the Joneses ................................... 7
CHAPTER 2: RETHINK Self-Assessment Quiz ...................... 25
CHAPTER 3: How to Make Changes ............................... 30
CHAPTER 4: Re-Create Your Vision ............................. 38
   Secret of Money #1: Make A Personal Commitment .. 40
   Secret of Money #2: Your Ten-Year Vision ............... 43
   Secret of Money #3: The Cost of Your Vision ........... 46
   Secret of Money #4: Creating Self-Trust ................ 50
   Secret of Money #5: The Financial Chase ................ 54
   Secret of Money #6: Today Is Your Future ............... 57
   Secret of Money #7: Your Flawed Thinking ............... 60
CHAPTER 5: Evaluate Where You Are ............................ 65
   Secret of Money #8: Evaluate Your Finances Using Your "HOMS" ............................................... 67
   Secret of Money #9: Your Personal Net Worth ........... 72
   Secret of Money #10: Facing Reality, Taking Responsibility ........................................... 75
   Secret of Money #11: Releasing the Past; Clearing Expectations ............................................. 78

- Secret of Money #12: Behavior Assessment ............... 81
- Secret of Money #13: Engage Your Ideal Behaviors .. 84
- Secret of Money #14: Put the Systems in Place .......... 87

CHAPTER 6: Target Your Income ............................... 90
- Secret of Money #15: Your HOMS on Cash Flow ...... 92
- Secret of Money #16: Prepare Your Cash Flow Statement ................................................................... 96
- Secret of Money #17: Under Earning ......................... 99
- Secret of Money #18: Creating Earning Power ......... 102
- Secret of Money #19: Leveraging Your Passion ....... 105
- Secret of Money #20: Letting Go ............................... 108
- Secret of Money #21: Skills, Passions and Making Money! ....................................................................... 111

CHAPTER 7: Harness Your Expenses ....................... 115
- Secret of Money #22: Harness Your Expenses .......... 117
- Secret of Money #23: Needs, Wants, Extras ............. 121
- Secret of Money #24: Spending Leaks ...................... 124
- Secret of Money #25: Decision Making .................... 127
- Secret of Money #26: Overcoming Mistakes ............ 130
- Secret of Money #27: Cash Flow Forecasting ........... 133
- Secret of Money #28: Willingness to Change ........... 136

CHAPTER 8: Integrate Your Assets ........................... 139
- Secret of Money #29: Integrate Your Assets ............. 141
- Secret of Money #30: Definition of Assets ............... 145
- Secret of Money #31: "Use" Assets ........................... 148

Secret of Money #32: Definition of Investments ........ 152

Secret of Money #33: What is "Enough"? ................ 155

Secret of Money #34: Flaws of Real Estate Ownership ................................................................. 158

Secret of Money #35: Get out of Denial! .................. 161

CHAPTER 9: Negate Your Liabilities ....................... **164**

Secret of Money #36: Negate Your Liabilities .......... 166

Secret of Money #37: Good Debt, Bad Debt ............ 169

Secret of Money #38: Debt vs. Leverage .................. 172

Secret of Money #39: Consumer Debt—A Cultural Change ................................................................. 175

Secret of Money #40: Investing in Education—Debt or Leverage? ............................................................ 178

Secret of Money #41: Spending Decisions ................ 182

Secret of Money #42: Be Patient and Consistent ....... 185

CHAPTER 10: Keep It All Safe! ............................... **187**

Secret of Money #43: Understanding Risks .............. 189

Secret of Money #44: You are the Biggest Risk ........ 192

Secret of Money #45: Protect Your HOMS ............... 195

Secret of Money #46: Start with Five-Year Goals ..... 198

Secret of Money #47: Create Your Six-Month Goals ................................................................. 201

Secret of Money #48: Next…Action Steps ............... 204

Secret of Money #49: Accountability ....................... 207

CHAPTER 11: On the Road to Success .................... **210**

ABOUT THE AUTHOR ......................................... **213**

# ACKNOWLEDGEMENTS

This book was written in 20 minutes per day, every day over the course of a few months, while drinking my morning coffee at the local coffee shop. Writing a book is no easy task—it just takes persistence, for which I owe many thanks to all my friends, family and mentors for helping me develop this skill.

Those who are exceptionally influential to me are: Gary Gottlieb my business advisor and friend, Steve Thomas my executive coach, Gary Ryan Blair (TheGoalsGuy) my business coach, Ellin Chess my spiritual life coach, Deborah Price my friend and mentor, Grace Brooke my professional organizer.

But I must mention how important the rest of my family and friends are; my mom, my kids Tom and Kim, and my close friends, who have been there for me to complain to and cry with, love and listen, fall apart and laugh with along the way.

And I especially want to acknowledge my gratitude for my Karate training and my instructor Sensei Cogen Bohanec

*For video coaching on the secrets and their corresponding Wealth Tools, go to www.49SecretsofMoney.com*

## 2 THE JONESES ARE BROKE!

(www.SonomaYogaMartialArts.com), who has been instrumental in my ability to complete this project. The philosophical, moral, and spiritual aspects of my karate training have contributed significantly to my personal development. One of the twenty principles of Shotokan Karate, *Niju Kun #10: Put Karate into Your Everyday Living—That is How to See Its True Beauty,* is a real testament to how the character development learned in Karate translates into cultivation of discipline, patience, diligence, humility and persistence necessary for the success and completion of this book.

And thank you to any other acquaintances or strangers who want to see this message open the door to changing the social norms around money.

*For video coaching on the secrets and their corresponding Wealth Tools, go to www.49SecretsofMoney.com*

# INTRODUCTION

Where was this information twenty years ago?

Good question! No, we didn't (nor do we now) teach in our schools how to have a fulfilling and satisfying life…one complete with jobs that utilize our natural skills, talents and passions, achieving all of our goals and legacies, while planning for the future and obtaining financial security. This is much more than financial education, this is about learning how <u>you</u>, an important individual, can make a difference in the world by knowing who you are, and how <u>you</u> can make an impact. Once you've discovered this, then you must learn the skills and behaviors necessary to use money to support yourself and your dreams, now and in the future, so that you can be highly successful as your best self.

Is financial education important? Absolutely! But financial education by itself will not get results. Actions get results. And knowing how to focus your actions in meaningful directions is critical. Once you've determined what a meaningful direction is for you, and you apply the

*For video coaching on the secrets and their corresponding Wealth Tools, go to www.49SecretsofMoney.com*

## 4 THE JONESES ARE BROKE!

combination of education and action…your chances of success will skyrocket.

This is so critical in understanding all the elements of financial success, because financial success has little to do with 'financial' and a lot to do with 'success'!

The 49 Secrets of Money will guide you through The Seven Keys to Financial Success. These seven critical areas of money that lead to financial success are:

**R**e-Create Your Vision

**E**valuate Where You Are

**T**arget Your Income

**H**arness Your Expenses

**I**ntegrate Your Assets

**N**egate Your Liabilities

**K**eep It All Safe!

But, before we get started, understanding what you are up against might help. Your current way of thinking is representative of decades of cultural thoughts and ideas that influence your thoughts, behaviors and fears. These

*For video coaching on the secrets and their corresponding Wealth Tools, go to www.49SecretsofMoney.com*

## INTRODUCTION 5

ideas keep you confused, stuck, frustrated, or just plain broke! You must be aware that it's not easy breaking free from the pack...but having the determination and persistence necessary to set yourself apart and start living your ideal life is invaluable!

But, let me forewarn you, the 49 Secrets of Money is not a quick fix program. It is not going to teach you how to become a millionaire next month. This is not a 'get rich quick' program, nor is it designed to get you out of immediate crisis. If you are in immediate financial crisis, you may need to speak to a bankruptcy attorney, a credit counselor or a therapist. However, if you are on the edge, tired of living paycheck to paycheck, are worried about retirement, or want to transition into a better life for yourself, then embarking on this journey through the 49 Secrets of Money is the best tool you'll find that will coach you, encourage you, be frank with you, and open your eyes to something more important and valuable than what you have today...peace with money.

What the 49 Secrets of Money program is designed to do, is to help you gain a new way of thinking about money, provide you with the tools you need to start making changes right now, and show you how to make changes in your life that will help you develop the discipline you need for long term success.

And you are not alone.

On our website, www.49secretsofmoney.com, you can purchase the video coaching program of the 49 Secrets of Money, in which I will personally walk you through each secret with a short 5-8 minute coaching video. Also, you'll

---

*For video coaching on the secrets and their corresponding Wealth Tools, go to www.49SecretsofMoney.com*

**6** THE JONESES ARE BROKE!

find access to seven Wealth Tools, which are the learning modules for each of the seven critical areas of money. These Wealth Tools teach you the 'how-to' steps with corresponding worksheets to deepen your learning, give you simple, easy to apply, tools and further support your long term success.

Okay, are you ready to get started?

# CHAPTER 1:
# Meet the Joneses

## Who are the Joneses?

Everyone in America, and probably throughout the world has heard of the "American Dream". The Dream of opportunity, choice, ability to work, material prosperity, equality and education. Our founding fathers planted the seed of the American Dream in the Declaration of Independence with words that meant freedom and opportunity:

> "...held certain truths to be self evident, that all Men are created equal, that they are endowed by their Creator with certain unalienable rights, that among these are life, Liberty and the Pursuit of Happiness."

But "pursuit" is also another word for "chase".

The phrase "keeping up with the Joneses" sums up the never-ending chase for the American Dream,; the key words being "the chase". But who are the Joneses? The Joneses represent the lifestyle, the material possessions, the "American Look"...everything that has not yet been purchased or achieved. The Joneses are the family next

---

*For video coaching on the secrets and their corresponding Wealth Tools, go to www.49SecretsofMoney.com*

# 8 THE JONESES ARE BROKE!

door, down the block, or in the next neighborhood. They are the family that is one or more steps ahead of where you are right now. The Joneses represent the next place, or stage in life, that you want to be in. Whether it's the faster car, the bigger house, the better clothes, the stronger power tools, or the best education, it's the representation of the next movement up the societal ladder.

The original phrase "keeping up with the Joneses" came from a comic strip created by Arthur R. "Pop" Momand that dates back as early as 1913. The comic strip started in newspapers and was eventually adapted into books, films, and musicals. But the Joneses in this comic strip were never actually seen, they were only referred to. By only referencing them, each reader could then impose their own version of the Joneses. But ironically, often when you talk about the Joneses, you are never referring to you or your friends and family. The Joneses are always someone else. Someone over there...somewhere. However, it's important to remember that you are the Joneses for someone else. Someone is looking to keep up with you. You are that for someone else, somewhere, and that's easy to forget.

## Why keep up with them?

There are actually two questions to consider in understanding this idea of "chasing the Joneses". The first question, "what does keeping up with them mean?", and the second, "why do you want to keep up with them?" Keeping up with the Joneses is really an attitude. It's an attitude of always striving; striving and always needing to get somewhere. It is wanting more...more convenience, more comfort, more security, more luxury, more sense of accomplishment. It's striving for social status. However, it is not actually "achieving status", because it doesn't stop at

*For video coaching on the secrets and their corresponding Wealth Tools, go to www.49SecretsofMoney.com*

achieving. There is no "there". It's never ending and it's never achieved.

So why do you want to keep up with them? Because often dissatisfaction with where you are and with what you have drives you to look elsewhere. Think about it. Imagine for a minute that your current life is okay. Imagine if right where you are, everything you have is perfectly fine. You don't want anything newer, better, or faster. Take a longer minute to think about it. At first, you might tell yourself, "yes, I'm fine. My life is great," but think longer. At first it's putting on the pretty face, the smile, the "I'm fine" expression. But ask yourself, "Am I really fine?" Then ask it again. Then again. Do you find that there is an underlying discontentment that starts to creep up? Is there a gnawing feeling of inadequacy, incompletion, or even boredom that creeps in when you stop for even just a moment? Maybe you are telling yourself you are fine because you don't want to face your frustration, of not being motivated to do what you know you really should do?

The underlying discomfort blinds you from seeing how much you already have. Even if it is not material things. In fact, it's not about the material things. But don't take this to mean accepting mediocrity! This means applying yourself in much more meaningful, impactful ways. Not in ways that accumulate stuff…in ways that demonstrate your ability to have a positive impact on the world. Society continues to use consumerism and material things to fulfill that discomfort, but in actuality, isn't accumulating things really about trying to fill that loneliness, emptiness, insecurity, and/or disappointment?

*For video coaching on the secrets and their corresponding Wealth Tools, go to www.49SecretsofMoney.com*

But it's also the lack of discipline and inability to say "no" to your wants that forces the search for true satisfaction. The cultural mindset is driven by an attitude of "we want what we want, and we want it now." Blindness and discontentment are reduced as values and long-term goals become more aligned with each other and better short-term financial choices are made. This builds when a new definition of success has been defined for your family and you apply the necessary discipline to take worthy steps toward it. The discipline required to say "no" to what you want <u>now</u> for something more valuable in the long-term is not only rewarding, it is liberating. It liberates you from the chase and liberates your heart to experience more life. This is the beginning of saying "no" to chasing the Joneses, and to discovering your own family milestones and definitions of success.

## Who are the Joneses REALLY?

By now you may still be questioning what's wrong with trying to keep up with the Joneses. You may be asking yourself, "what's wrong with trying to improve my life and my material acquisitions?" And I say, maybe nothing. Acquiring material things, building current and future security, and enjoying the material things in life can be fun and rewarding. All I suggest is to ask yourself a few meaningful questions, such as "how do you feel about your financial situation?", "how's your relationship with your significant other?", "what's money doing for you?", "how's your communication regarding money?", "do you love your job?", "does money hurt?", "what are your biggest concerns about money?", and especially, "are you happy?"

---

*For video coaching on the secrets and their corresponding Wealth Tools, go to www.49SecretsofMoney.com*

I wonder what the answers to some of these questions might be for the Joneses? What do the Joneses feel about their financial situation? Imagine that you've just pulled up to the front of the Joneses home (parked in front of the white picket fence), and you've brought your spy gear to listen in on their conversation and your binoculars to zoom into their front window. It's 9:00pm and the 2.5 kids have just brushed their teeth (yes, with whitening toothpaste) and headed blissfully to bed after helping clean the kitchen, taking out the trash, happily turning off the TV and completing all their homework. (Okay, I won't get too fairytale...but isn't this a taste of what we are actually comparing our families to—or at least expecting that it should be like that?)

So, mom and dad sit down at the dining room table to talk about their money, and what happens? A happy, loving, playful conversation about money that discusses their current balance sheet, their cash flow statement, their progress towards their goals, the ease with which money comes in and goes out, and how much they love how money enhances their relationship and brings great fulfillment, closeness, and liberation to their family? NOT! What might you really see? Silence? Confusion? Discomfort? Anger? Disappointment? Arguing? Fear? Stress? Blame? Guilt? Shame? Embarrassment? In reality, the conversation may sound more like,

> "Did you transfer the money into the savings account today, honey?"

> "No, there wasn't any money to transfer. I looked at the balance in the account, and the money's not there. What did you do with it?"

*For video coaching on the secrets and their corresponding Wealth Tools, go to www.49SecretsofMoney.com*

## 12 THE JONESES ARE BROKE!

"What did I do with it? I don't take out money from the accounts, I use the charge cards. You're the one who's always writing the checks, paying the bills, and using the ATM. I thought we were trying to save money; why can't you make sure to put money into the savings account?"

"Because there isn't any money there to put into the savings account! By the time I pay all the bills and the credit cards, department stores, the cable, phone, cell phone, internet, car payment, and house payments, there's nothing left! You've got to stop charging on the accounts if you want to us to be able to save! When will you start listening to me? Money doesn't grow on trees you know!"

"I wouldn't have to charge on the cards if you would just…"

This could go on and on, with the tension building (caused by a lack of understanding and communication about the family money) and finally the release by throwing blame, frustration, anger, etc. Even if there's plenty of money, similar conversations (or arguments) break out regarding whether to buy the next car, or boat, or airplane, or new house, or whatever.

Is there ever enough when you always want more?

By the time the "real Joneses" go to bed, they may have let their emotions loose around their pent up money troubles. Maybe one spouse takes care of all the money and deposits an allowance for the other, so no talking is ever "needed" and any thoughts, ideas, or feelings about money can easily be swept under the rug. Or perhaps one spouse is out of work and unable to bring in an adequate amount of money, so the conversation teeters on shame and inadequacy. Or one spouse can't stop shopping or gambling and knows that it's destroying their finances, but can't stop the habit and is filled with guilt, denial and self loathing—while the other spouse is bursting with anger, frustration, and hopelessness.

Some of these financial patterns I've nicknamed over the years as Financial Anorexia, Financial Bulimia, and Financial Obesity. Whether it's starving yourself from money, overspending your money, or hoarding money, many of the feelings associated with these patterns can cause devastation not only to the finances, but also to the relationship and to yourself.

So, by being honest with yourself about how the Joneses might REALLY be feeling, behaving, and communicating, it might shed some light on the reality of who the Joneses really are (or aren't), and question your true desire to really be more like them.

## Why are they broke?
Besides the emotional side of the Joneses, what about the reality of their financial life? Are they as wealthy and free as you think they are? For the average American Joneses family, let's say they have a 3 bedroom/2 bath house, 2 cars, 2 kids, 2 jobs, 1 boat, 1 golf club membership, 4 credit cards, 4 cell phones, 2 computers, 2 flat screen TV's, weekly soccer, ballet, football, piano, violin, T-ball, gymnastics, martial arts, birthday parties, Girl/Boy Scouts,

4H, …(okay, I could go on and on with all the activities we busy our kids' lives with, but I won't). Anyway, if we looked at their balance sheet and their cash flow statement, would they be financially free? Hardly…financially burdened more likely (not even accounting the devastating effects of the housing and credit crises!). The truth is, most of us don't even know what our balance sheet and cash flow statements are or how to use them. Corporations rely on them to determine the outcome of their strategic and operational strategies, plan for their upcoming cash needs, and monitor their financial position, but as individuals we are far from understanding how to do this and why it's important.

Let's take the simple case of the average American Joneses family above. They might have a balance sheet that looks like this:

## Assets (Market Value)

| | |
|---|---|
| House | $400,000 |
| Cars | $45,000 |
| Jewelry, Furnishings & TVs | $30,000 |
| Boat | $15,000 |
| Motorcycle | $20,000 |
| Retirement Accounts | $50,000 |
| Savings & Checking | $5,000 |
| | **$565,000** |

## Liabilities

| | |
|---|---|
| House | $395,000 |
| Cars | $60,000 |
| Credit Cards | $20,000 |
| Boat | $20,000 |
| Motorcycle | $15,000 |
| 401k Loan | $25,000 |
| Department Stores | $15,000 |
| | **$550,000** |
| **Net Worth** | **$15,000** |

---

*For video coaching on the secrets and their corresponding Wealth Tools, go to www.49SecretsofMoney.com*

# 16 THE JONESES ARE BROKE!

With all that they "have"—they really have very little. They owe nearly as much as they have. And in many households, they owe more than they have. The critical factor in their finances is their cash flow. Are they spending more than they're earning? If they are, their liabilities will increase and their net worth will continue to shrink. If they're not, their liabilities will shrink, their assets will grow, and their net worth will increase if they don't continually spend the excess on new increases in lifestyle and more monthly expenses.

## What happened?

Over the last five decades, not only had the US average household debt been increasing, the US average savings rate had been decreasing as well, with it reaching its lowest before the financial crisis of 2008 and actually going negative. This means that for every dollar earned, Americans were spending on average $1.25. These are indicators that the average American Joneses family's net worth had been shrinking for a long time.

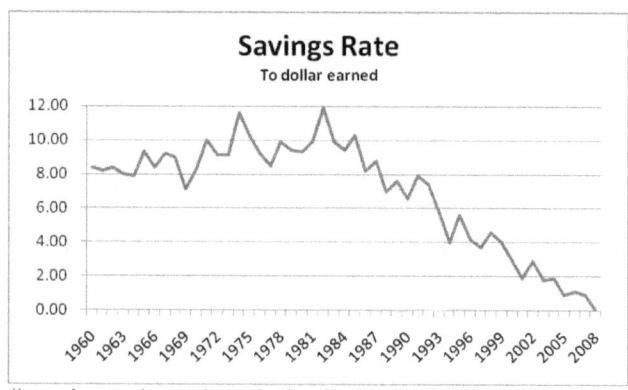

http://www.bea.gov/newsreleases/national/pi/2010/pdf/pi0710.pdf

*For video coaching on the secrets and their corresponding Wealth Tools, go to www.49SecretsofMoney.com*

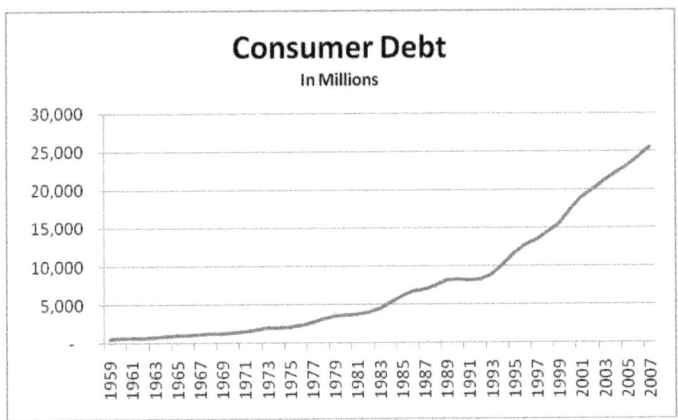

http://www.federalreserve.gov/releases/g19/hist/cc_hist_mt.html

With the savings rates plunging and the consumer debt skyrocketing, the final attempt and keeping up with the Joneses came from home equity. Using homes as an ATM machine, American's began covering their overspending by borrowing against the equity in their homes.

Ending this fifty year overspending, over borrowing frenzy, the economy came to a screeching halt with the financial crisis starting in 2008.

With American's, and the rest of the world reeling into a panic, in the last three months of 2008 there was a sudden reversal of the debt and savings patterns, and for the first time in American history, more debt was paid off than was incurred, and the savings rate jumped into the positive overnight.

## 18 THE JONESES ARE BROKE!

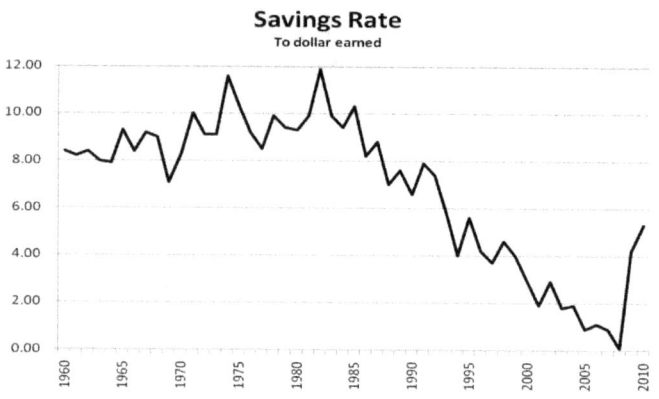

*For video coaching on the secrets and their corresponding Wealth Tools, go to www.49SecretsofMoney.com*

# CHAPTER 1: MEET THE JONESES 19

However, this radical change may not be enough to change old patterns when there is still an old mindset.

For comparison, let's look at the bankruptcy filings (next chart). In 2005 the rates dropped significantly, not due to a change in behavior, but due to a change in the law. This outside influence only caused a temporary change in filings, but as you can see, five years later, the number of filings has surpassed the rate prior to the passing of the law. This doesn't indicate a lasting change of behavior! In fact, it doesn't even indicate a short term change in behavior. It was purely due to external factors.

And this is exactly the concern that I'm pointing out with the changes in the savings rates and consumer debt statistics. Will American's use this opportunity to gain the skills needed, change their thinking, and start new behaviors that will be sustainable beyond the crisis? Or will we go back to old pattern with the first sign of an improved economy?

## Are the Joneses headed for bankruptcy?

In order to sustain increasing debt rates and decreasing savings rates, the money that is spent on consumerism has to come from somewhere. Once you increase your debt in excess of your savings, you begin eroding your net worth.

As I've mentioned, eroding savings and home equity leaves more debt and less assets. It is inevitable that increasing debt and decreasing savings leads to bankruptcy. According to the American Bankruptcy Institute, the total number of US bankruptcies filed during the first six months of 2007 increased 48% over the same period in

*For video coaching on the secrets and their corresponding Wealth Tools, go to www.49SecretsofMoney.com*

## 20 THE JONESES ARE BROKE!

2006, and as of the second quarter of 2008, they were up another 29%.

By the end of 2010, the personal bankruptcy rates have doubled those of 2006!

It's no wonder that since the introduction of the first plastic credit card in 1959, America's debt immediately increased, and so did its ensuing problems and mindset.

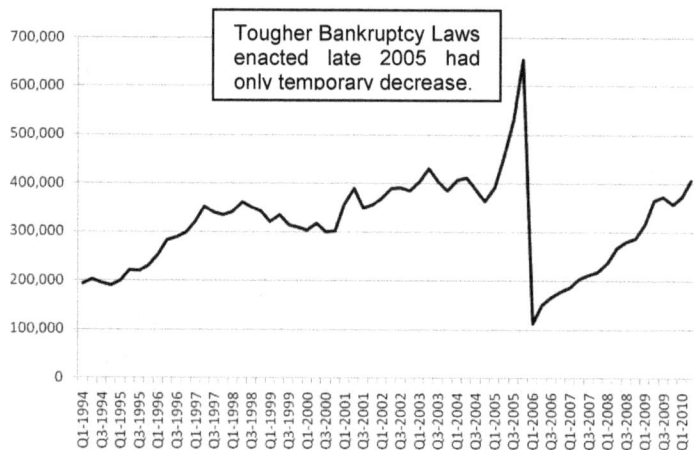

**Personal Bankruptcy Filings**
Since 1994

http://www.abiworld.org/AM/AMTemplate.cfm?Section=Home&TEMPLATE=/CM/ContentDisplay.cfm&CONTENTID=57800

But the problem of bankruptcies occurring at increasingly rapid rates is especially alarming in our baby boomer and aging populations. According to the 2007 Consumer

Bankruptcy Project[1], the bankruptcy rates from 1991-2007 for those between 55-64 had increased by 40%, those aged 65-74 by 125% and most alarmingly, those between 75-84 had increased by 433%!

Over the years, the desire has been lost, and maybe even the ability, to manage and monitor finances based on long-term goals. This has stemmed from years of being able to buy and do what you want when you want without having to worry about it. Over the last 50 years, credit has been easy to obtain and easy to use. Think about it, Gen X and Gen Y's have always had easy access to credit, and more and more are no longer using (or have never used) a checkbook. One analogy that makes sense is the comparison of allowing the water hose to run while you are washing the car. If you lived in the severe drought years in Australia (or even California), you would think twice about making sure the hose had a nozzle to keep the water off when you're not rinsing the car. Or better yet, you may not even wash your car in the summer! But would you worry about it in the same way if you were washing your car in Seattle, where it rains most of the year?

I'm sure the Joneses have also noticed they are broke, and possibly heading for bankruptcy, but what can they do to turn it around? With no personal finance training in schools and poor communication at home, there have been few resources available to learn how to develop the discipline

---

[1] In 2007, several Harvard scholars sought out to assess the impact of the legislation's change in bankruptcy laws and their effectiveness, and to measure what effects, if any, the legislation had on bankruptcy for families and consumers. This group produced reports and studies commonly referred to as the "Consumer Bankruptcy Project.

and skills needed to grow a healthy net worth and achieve long-term goals, especially with all the electronic changes in today's money system.

> *Remember, if you are not saving for the future, then you are not living within your means.*

The shame and embarrassment of not being able to address the problems and keep up with the Joneses allows denial to continue to bury the problem and dig the hole deeper. So they wake up one day, wondering "what happened?", and are blindsided by the financial problem that has turned into a family crisis, often leading to bankruptcy, foreclosure, divorce and chaos.

## Why rethink financial success?

A new definition of financial success is necessary because the current way of thinking about and using money is broken and it cannot last. As seen from the results of the tech boom (and bust) and the real estate boom (and bust), our finance system itself is in crisis. This has been the worst decade in history for our financial markets, with cash outperforming stocks. Another serious problem is the growing fiscal irresponsibility in our governments. The amount of debt incurred and the increased overspending by our governments is also a demonstration of the level of tolerance for overspending that each individual has and is just a reflection of our own personal overspending.

If each of us took the personal steps necessary to become more fiscally responsible and spending within their means, there would be no tolerance for the level of debt the governments are creating.

Take a look at the U.S. National Debt Clock:

> **U.S. NATIONAL DEBT CLOCK**
> The Outstanding Public Debt as of 21 Feb 2011 at 12:54:02 AM GMT is:
>
> **$14,136,486,666,473.62**

http://www.brillig.com/debt_clock/

These numbers are hard to comprehend. If you laid dollar bills end to end, one trillion dollars would stretch nearly from the Earth to the Sun. That means you'd have to multiply that by 14 to get to the 14 trillion dollars of debt. And this doesn't even account for the interest on that debt!

In February 2009, the national debt was $10.8 trillion. That means that in less than one year, <u>the national debt has risen over 30%</u>!

Since September of 2007, the national debt has risen on average over $4.2 billion dollars per day!

But that's just the federal government. The states are also in debt and don't have viable plans to repay that debt either.

Obviously, the problem is serious, yet there would be less tolerance for it if every individual began to think differently about money and build a solid financial plan based on values, and financial practices that create stability and self reliance; not on "keeping up with the Joneses."

---

*For video coaching on the secrets and their corresponding Wealth Tools, go to www.49SecretsofMoney.com*

> *Instead of white picket fences, why not a new American Dream of long term sustainability.*

It's not just the overspending, the lack of savings, and the fiscal aspects that create the need to rethink financial success. It's the lack of peace that's creating substantial damage. Being at peace with money comes from being personally responsible, being accountable, being disciplined, and using money to further your values. It also comes from gaining an understanding of your finances and learning new tools to plan for your future.

A new definition of success can open the idea of slowing down spending and thinking twice about your wants. Slow down and think about your true wants and needs. Slow down and spend time instead of money to create less stress. Use time in ways that invigorate you, motivate you, energize you, and allow you to create meaning in your life.

In order to make long-term, lasting changes in your life and in society, you must change some of your underlying assumptions about how you currently use money. Begin to talk comfortably about money without shame, fear, judgment or embarrassment and use money to enhance ALL of your relationships, not tear them down. When you take the right steps in your own personal life, your resulting power can change the rest of the world through your becoming a role model and inspiring others to live up to your example…especially your children and the next generation.

*For video coaching on the secrets and their corresponding Wealth Tools, go to www.49SecretsofMoney.com*

# CHAPTER 2:
# RETHINK Self-Assessment Quiz

Before going into the seven critical areas and the 49 Secrets of Money, start with the following self-assessment quiz. By taking the following self-assessment quiz, you'll gain an understanding of your strengths and weaknesses and be able to identify which areas will have the biggest impact on creating peace in your financial life. By starting with an assessment, you will be creating a new awareness about money and a new perspective on your current situation.

For each question below, indicate on a scale of 0 to 7 where you are today.

---

*For video coaching on the secrets and their corresponding Wealth Tools, go to www.49SecretsofMoney.com*

# 26 THE JONESES ARE BROKE!

|   |   | Always Very | | | | | | Never, Don't None Know |
|---|---|---|---|---|---|---|---|---|
| | score | 7 | 6 | 5 | 4 | 3 | 2 | 1 | 0 |

| # | Statement | Score |
|---|---|---|
| 1 | For my age today, I am happy with what I've accomplished in my financial life. | ○ ○ ○ ○ ○ ○ ○ ○ |
| 2 | I am actively living my life in a meaningful direction that matches my true passions. | ○ ○ ○ ○ ○ ○ ○ ○ |
| 3 | My assets & investments are adequately allocated to meet my safety, leisure & future needs. | ○ ○ ○ ○ ○ ○ ○ ○ |
| 4 | I review my net worth and the progress I've made toward my goals at least annually. | ○ ○ ○ ○ ○ ○ ○ ○ |
| 5 | I am pleased with how I use my money, and how it affects my long-term goals. | ○ ○ ○ ○ ○ ○ ○ ○ |
| 6 | I am satisfied with my credit score and my ability to manage debt to get my goals. | ○ ○ ○ ○ ○ ○ ○ ○ |
| 7 | I am at peace with money most of the time, and worry very little about my finances. | ○ ○ ○ ○ ○ ○ ○ ○ |
| 8 | My spending is appropriately balanced between my needs, wants, and extras. | ○ ○ ○ ○ ○ ○ ○ ○ |

*For video coaching on the secrets and their corresponding Wealth Tools, go to www.49SecretsofMoney.com*

# CHAPTER 2: RETHINK SELF-ASSESSMENT QUIZ

|  |  | Iway:/Very | | | | | | Never Don't/None Know |
|---|---|---|---|---|---|---|---|---|
|  | score | 7 | 6 | 5 | 4 | 3 | 2 | 1 | 0 |
| 9 | I am confident that I am on the right track and will be able to achieve all my goals. | ○ | ○ | ○ | ○ | ○ | ○ | ○ | ○ |
| 10 | I know how to use my personal balance sheet and to gauge its strength (or lack there of). | ○ | ○ | ○ | ○ | ○ | ○ | ○ | ○ |
| 11 | I am willing to spend time & effort on learning & readjusting my finances to improve my future. | ○ | ○ | ○ | ○ | ○ | ○ | ○ | ○ |
| 12 | I am confident that the amount of risk I take with my assets, is the right amount. | ○ | ○ | ○ | ○ | ○ | ○ | ○ | ○ |
| 13 | I feel in complete control of my household spending, saving and investing. | ○ | ○ | ○ | ○ | ○ | ○ | ○ | ○ |
| 14 | I usually enjoy my job, feel fully utilized, and feel adequately paid. | ○ | ○ | ○ | ○ | ○ | ○ | ○ | ○ |
| 15 | I am satisfied that all my assets are successfully helping me reach my long-term goals. | ○ | ○ | ○ | ○ | ○ | ○ | ○ | ○ |
| 16 | I understand the difference between debt & leverage and manage my liabilities accordingly. | ○ | ○ | ○ | ○ | ○ | ○ | ○ | ○ |

*For video coaching on the secrets and their corresponding Wealth Tools, go to www.49SecretsofMoney.com*

# 28 THE JONESES ARE BROKE!

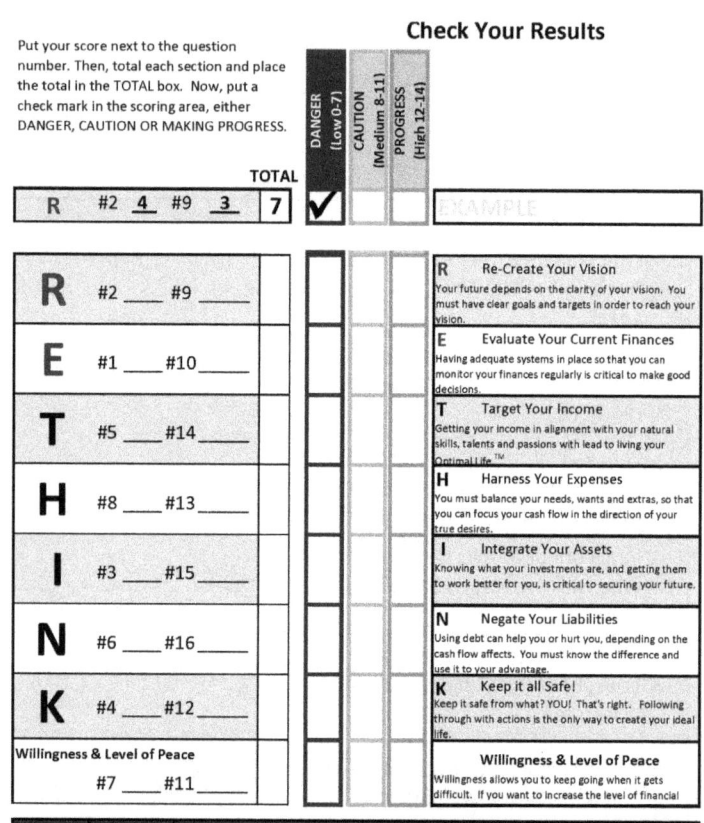

If you didn't do as well as you might have thought, or if you scored unpleasantly low, don't worry, you're not alone. Almost everyone I've seen take the quiz was unhappy with the results. But there is good news! You can improve your scores quickly with small steps. Completely changing your whole financial picture may take a while,

*For video coaching on the secrets and their corresponding Wealth Tools, go to www.49SecretsofMoney.com*

but feeling better about the direction you're headed, and understanding what needs to be done to get there, will instantly give you more satisfaction.

But, it's going to take a real commitment to looking at your life and changing your behaviors. Remember, if your current behaviors didn't need to change...you probably wouldn't be reading this right now. What you know has gotten you where you are, now it's time for new skills, new ideas and a new approach.

Keep going through each secret, taking your time to do the Action steps as best you can. I suggest you take the quiz again after you've completed all the secrets, or the 49 Secrets of Money on-line coaching program. I'm sure you'll see a great improvement already.

# CHAPTER 3:
# How to Make Changes

## 5 Steps for Changing Financial Behaviors

In order to make successful changes in your behavior, becoming aware of the change process ahead of time eliminates surprises as you are going through the process.

There are five steps in the financial change process. If you stay with these steps, you will have a higher likelihood to not only making the changes you want, but also in keeping them for the long term!

## CHAPTER 3: HOW TO MAKE CHANGES  31

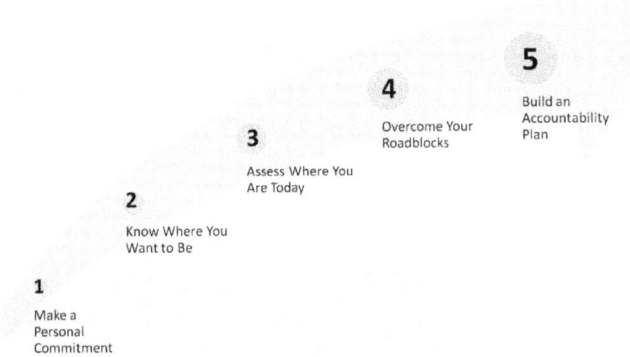

The first step is to make a personal commitment. This is a commitment to yourself, to your progress and to your success.

It is NOT a commitment to a task. It is a commitment to the type of person you want to become. Making a strong commitment will be a good reminder as to why you're doing all this in the first place.

The next step is NOT to assess where you are, but to define where you want to be...your ideal future. This is important to do <u>before</u> you assess where you are, so that you are anchored in something meaningful that inspires you when times get rough. Then, and only then, must you learn how to accurately assess where you are, both in financial terms and behavioral terms! This takes real courage to honestly reveal and face your financial situation. It also takes facing the reality that maybe you don't even know where to start. As uncomfortable as it may feel, it is that you have this

*For video coaching on the secrets and their corresponding Wealth Tools, go to www.49SecretsofMoney.com*

type of willingness, because that means you are ready to learn!

The fourth step is to overcome your roadblocks. Roadblocks will always show up, but you must learn to recognize them early, and make changes so that they don't stop your progress. There are four common road blocks:

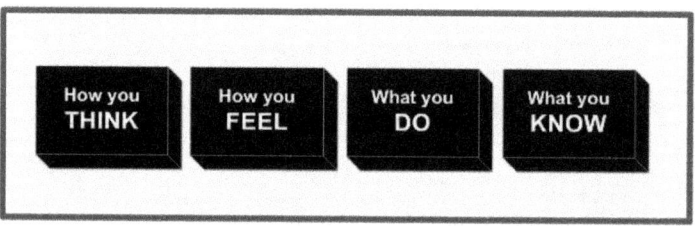

The way you think about money, the way you feel about money, what you do with money (your habits), and what you know about how money works (your skills) will all get in your way at some point if you let them. Learning how to recognize when your feelings are driving your decisions, for example, can give you time to react differently, and make a better choice.

Once you've mastered all these, then the last step is creating an accountability plan for yourself to stay on track and on task! An accountability plan means following through with what you say you'll do. It means putting measures in place that help you build discipline and personal accountability. As this happens, you confidence grows, and so does your success!

This change process is continual and ongoing. It never stops. Gaining the tools to quickly and objectively change your behaviors is a lifelong skill that will lead to success in all areas of your life. Each of these skills is addressed throughout the rest of the 49 Secrets of Money.

## The Seven Keys to Financial Success and the 49 Secrets of Money

In all aspects of financial success, it is vitally important to first master the simple, easy to understand concepts of cash flow and net worth. In the 49 Secrets of Money, these are taught through a concept called your HOMS to address a simple way of understanding cash flow and net worth.

Your HOMS stands for:

What You **HAVE**

What You **OWE**

What You **MAKE**

What You **SPEND**

---

*For video coaching on the secrets and their corresponding Wealth Tools, go to www.49SecretsofMoney.com*

In order to determine your net worth, you must subtract what you owe, from what you have. What's left over is your net worth. Net worth is the amount of wealth you have at a given point in time.

# CHAPTER 3: HOW TO MAKE CHANGES

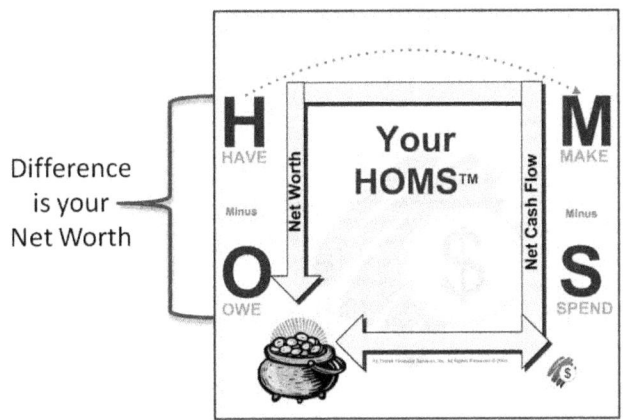

The ultimate goal is to build your assets, reduce your debt and increase your net worth so that you have the security you desire. Security comes from understanding how much net worth you need to support your future cash flow needs. This is the essence of financial planning: making sure you have a plan, and the resources, to cover your future cash needs.

As you build up assets that produce income, the income will flow over to the MS side and increase your cash flow. As long as you don't increase your spending, your cash flow will improve, and you'll have more cash available to either pay off debt or increase your assets.

To determine your cash flow, subtract what you spend from what you make. What's left over is your cash flow. Cash flow is the flow of money coming in and out during a given time period. If you have more money coming in than going out, you will have positive cash flow. If you spend

*For video coaching on the secrets and their corresponding Wealth Tools, go to www.49SecretsofMoney.com*

more than what's coming in, then you have negative cash flow.

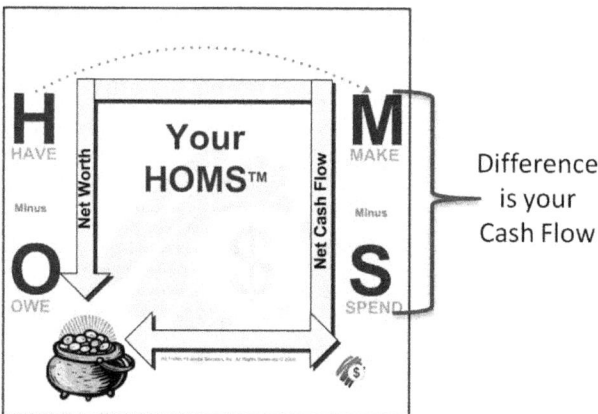

The goal is always to increase your cash flow. If it's negative now, make a goal to get it positive. When it's positive then make a goal to increase it even more. Positive cash flow will increase your net worth by either paying off debt or increasing your assets. Negative cash flow decreases your net worth and can eventually lead to bankruptcy.

You will continue to learn more about your HOMS in the 49 Secrets of Money, and about the importance of managing your cash flow to grow your wealth.

Just keep this in mind: you will gain financial security and become wealthier, as you master your cash flow and increase your net worth.

## CHAPTER 3: HOW TO MAKE CHANGES 37

Mastering your HOMS is mastering the flow of wealth into your pockets...instead of out of your pockets. It is the creation of wealth.

Your HOMS is embedded within the context of the seven critical areas of money, the R.E.T.H.I.N.K. areas known as The Seven Keys to Financial Success.

The 49 Secrets of Money is the breakdown of these Seven Keys that allows you to gain all the tools you need for long-term success and provides you with the information you need to create a simple, doable, short-term financial plan. Each chapter breaks these critical areas of money into seven secrets that covers in more detail all the elements you need to increase your skills.

So, before you get started, make sure you have a notebook handy for taking notes and for completing the exercises at the end of each secret. These secrets will prompt you to take action and encourage you to start making changes in your life <u>today</u>!

# CHAPTER 4:
# Re-Create Your Vision

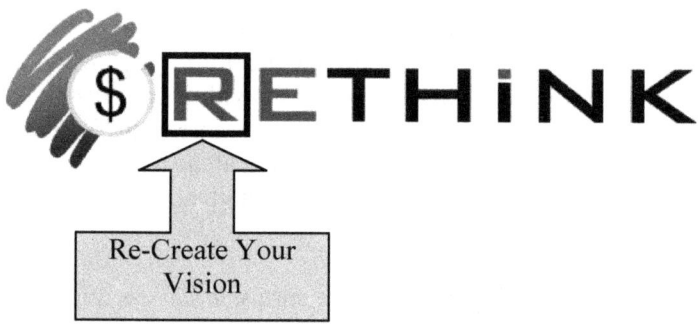

Imagine yourself driving down the highway on the coast on a warm, sunny day. Your seat reclined, one hand on the steering wheel, radio blasting, and your best friend sitting next to you shouting silly jokes over the music.
You are relaxed, having a good time.

Suddenly, around the next bend, you hit a thick fog bank and can hardly see 10 feet in front of you. What do you do?

Immediately slow down, maybe turn down the radio, grab the steering wheel with both hands and sit up straight.

When the road ahead of you is clear you can relax and enjoy the ride. When the vision for your life is clear, you can relax and enjoy yourself.

---

*For video coaching on the secrets and their corresponding Wealth Tools, go to www.49SecretsofMoney.com*

You can re-create your future by creating a clear vision. If you don't have one, it's time to get one. If you have one, maybe it's time to seriously re-create it so that you can have a real shot at having the future you desire.

As you begin your journey, you may find it difficult to know what you want. This is common. I've struggled many times trying to figure out what I really want, and just when I think I've got a clear idea, it changes.

The first time I went to talk to a financial advisor, she basically told me to "go figure out what you want, save up some money, and once you've done that, I'll help you invest it". This did me absolutely no good, in fact I left her office and sat in my car and cried for almost an hour. I was so lost. I didn't know how to figure out what I wanted and I didn't know where to go to get help. Who would help me, if a financial planner couldn't? In addition, I didn't even know how to save for my future, especially while I was living paycheck to paycheck.

But, as I quickly discovered....it wasn't her job to help me figure out what I wanted. Nor was it her job to get my money in order so I could actually start saving.

Going through struggles like this however, can be used to motivate you to take action. So if you find yourself confused, or uncertain, don't worry. There tools to help you, including our on-line coaching modules, the Wealth Tools, our Money Coaches and other resources that can help you gain the clarity you need.

## Secret of Money #1:
## Make A Personal Commitment

Nothing changes unless you are committed to seeing it change. If you want to quit smoking, a firm commitment to being a non-smoker is essential. If you want to be a martial artist, then a firm commitment to your training is essential. Without a commitment that you can fall back on, what will keep you on track when it gets uncomfortable?

### Learn

In order to get started, you must first ask yourself, "Why am I doing this?" Yes, I know, you want to improve your money situation and perhaps get some answers to some gnawing questions. But why do you want that?

If your money situation were exactly the way you wanted it to be, what would that be like? Would you have more happiness, more time with your family, more enjoyment out of life? Would your relationships be improved?

In order to gain the peace, relaxation and happiness around money that you are looking for, you will need to make changes. Perhaps changes in the way you think, the way you act, and the way you live. These changes will all be discovered throughout the next 49 Secrets. But first, you must make a personal commitment to your success.

A personal commitment is the promise that you make to yourself that will encourage you along the way. It is a statement about what's important to you. It goes "clunk" in your gut when you make a strong commitment that you know you will keep. Don't make a commitment that you know you won't keep. Don't kid yourself. Make it simple, doable, and one that goes "clunk."

This is not about short-term commitment to actions such as, "I commit to saving $100 a week." This is about a much truer commitment to yourself. For example, "I commit to becoming educated about money, to stopping habits that sabotage my efforts, and to using money in ways that build wealth and self trust."

> Don't wait another day, another minute, because you can't afford to.

This type of commitment is for life. Your life!

## Act

**Make Your Personal Commitment:**

In your notebook, jot down the answers that come to mind when you ask yourself;

1. Why am I doing this program?

2. How do I want my efforts to enhance my life and my relationships?

3. How willing am I to face uncomfortable money areas and make changes anyway?

*For video coaching on the secrets and their corresponding Wealth Tools, go to www.49SecretsofMoney.com*

These answers will help you formulate your commitment statement.

To make your commitment statement, summarize your thoughts and formulate a short statement that starts as:

In order to increase the amount of peace I have with money, to take action toward my goals, and to complete this 49 Secrets of Money program, I commit to:

___

Keep your commitment short and to the point. If it's too long, circle the verbs and look at the action words. Write your commitment on 3x5 cards, Post-Its, etc. and place them on your car visor, your wallet, your refrigerator, or wherever you'll see these daily reminders.

### Remember

> It's doing what you SAY you'll do that brings true satisfaction in life!

## Secret of Money #2: Your Ten-Year Vision

If you want financial happiness, you must take actions to get it...today. In order to achieve what you desire, you must stop doing what hurts you, and start doing what will bring you great success... one moment at a time. You must change the way you think about money, and you must change your behaviors.

### Learn

What is it that you truly want, anyway? Have you ever sat back and *really* dreamed?

A few years ago, I took a teenager to a clinic to expose her to the consequences of where her current actions could lead her.

At the start of the visit, the counselor asked her what she wanted her life to look like at age 27. This was very powerful, because if she wanted a house, happy marriage, cars, and so forth, she would have to ask herself if the young "man" she was seeing would be capable of supporting that lifestyle. What about the education they would need to increase wages? What about saving for a home or other large purchases? Would they be able to get there if they dropped out of high school, or had children too young?

It pointed out the importance of thinking ahead. It reinforced the value of really looking at what she wanted and what she would sacrifice if she made poor choices today.

Although she was headed down a rocky road, after really thinking about what she wanted for her future, she turned her life around, graduated from high school, went into the service, married and is now raising two happy, healthy children.

Now, imagine for yourself, taking a Sunday drive without any particular destination in mind. You are well on your way when you <u>finally</u> make a decision about where to go. You decide to go visit your mother-in-law (if that *ever* happens, right?), which happens to be up north. You may have headed 50 miles south and now have to completely change direction and add a lot of extra time onto your trip.

Knowing your destination ahead of time will get you there much faster. It's critical to know yourself, your dreams, and what makes your ideal life. How will you know what you need to do if you don't know where you want to be?

## Act

**Design Your Ten-Year Vision:**

In your notebook draw a large circle and divide the circle into eight sections.

Name each section: My Finances, My Living Situation, My Work/Career, My Family & Relationships, My Recreation/Leisure, My Health/Fitness, My Hobbies, and My Community.

*For video coaching on the secrets and their corresponding Wealth Tools, go to www.49SecretsofMoney.com*

For each area: take a few moments and write down what it is you *really want* in each of these areas. Write what your ideal life would look like in each area. This is the beginning of your ten-year vision.

**Remember**

> You can have anything you want... You just can't have everything you want!

## Secret of Money #3:
## The Cost of Your Vision

Imagine what it would feel like if you had $1 million dollars in the bank. If you can't, you don't have the capacity to receive it, and therefore you probably won't get it. If you're living in a poverty mindset, dreaming about becoming wealthy, stop dreaming! Get up and learn! Find out what the difference between a poverty mindset and a wealthy mindset is, and find out what you need to do to change it.

### Learn

Think about how you felt after you wrote down your ideal life in each of the eight areas in Secret #2. If you didn't complete that exercise, do so now. Envisioning your ideal life brings you to a place of relaxation, doesn't it?

But what was it that was most important about your ten-year vision? Was it the dollars? Was it a feeling? In your ideal life, what was most important to you—family life? Slow pace? Adventure? Playfulness?

If you thought money was the biggest factor, it might be time to rethink what you value. Understanding what's behind those dollars is what's critical. Just having the amount of money you think you want won't get you your ideal life.

*For video coaching on the secrets and their corresponding Wealth Tools, go to www.49SecretsofMoney.com*

## CHAPTER 4: RE-CREATE YOUR VISION 47

Being clear on what's really important and incorporating your daily actions in the right direction is how you gain that feeling of success.

But let's make it about the numbers for a minute. Let's talk about how your vision would translate into numbers by creating a Personal Net Worth statement (PNW). A Personal Net Worth statement is a list of everything that you have (your assets), minus everything that you owe (your liabilities). What's left over is your net worth.

> *Take a retreat. Go to the country or the beach and take some serious time to plan your life.*

Now I know in this economy you're lucky if you have *anything* left over—oftentimes when people are starting their mastery of money journey they start upside-down—owing more than they have.

But, let's stay in the dream for now.

The bottom line is, financial planning is the ability to test whether your net worth is "big enough" to do the job you intend for it—or not. If you are upside-down, your first goal should be to get your net worth positive. Then begin to plan how to create a large enough net worth to support your ideal life. Later in the Secrets you will learn how to get started on making this happen.

Before you calculate your actual Personal Net Worth, which we'll get to in the next couple of Secrets, let's start by creating a Personal Net Worth statement for your ideal

---

*For video coaching on the secrets and their corresponding Wealth Tools, go to www.49SecretsofMoney.com*

life. This is a good starting point for envisioning how the numbers would look if you were living your ideal life. It may be difficult to imagine the numbers, and you may have a limited capacity right now to receive the wealth you desire. But that will be addressed in the future...go for it anyway!

Remember, it's what's <u>behind</u> the numbers that will drive you toward success.

## Act

### Create Your "Ideal Life - Personal Net Worth Statement":

Take out and review your ten-year vision from Secret #2. Now, make a list of what your IDEAL assets would be. How much would you have in checking? Savings? Investments? Real estate? Business ownership? And so on, if you we living your ideal life. Now list any liabilities you are willing to have to obtain these assets. Remember, this is your ideal life...your dream.

Subtract the total liabilities from the total assets. This is what your net worth could look like if you had your Ideal Life."

How do you know if your Personal Net Worth is enough?

Even in with your Ideal Net Worth, you would need to understand how long your ideal life could be supported by this amount of net worth. Here's a down and dirty test.

    1. How much per month would it cost you to sustain that dream lifestyle? $_____.

## CHAPTER 4: RE-CREATE YOUR VISION 49

2. Now, if you sold all your assets and paid off all your debt and your leftover cash was piled on the table, how many months would it support?

   To find out: divide your net worth (from your Ideal Life Personal Net Worth statement) by your monthly lifestyle cost (in #1 above). The answer is the number of months your Ideal Life Personal Net Worth would support your dream lifestyle.

So here's the important point. Even in your ideal life…do you have enough?

### Remember

**Will you ever have enough when you're looking for something that can't be quantified?**

*For video coaching on the secrets and their corresponding Wealth Tools, go to www.49SecretsofMoney.com*

## Secret of Money #4: Creating Self Trust

In this Secret I may be a little harsh on you, but not because I don't care. It's because I do care. I care a lot.

I just want to get an important point across.

When you don't follow through with things, your actions are untrustworthy. No one likes to admit to themselves that they are not trustworthy. But if you are not taking actions in the direction you want to be headed, then you are not being trustworthy. You are not doing what you say you'll do. Become impeccable with your word by saying only what you'll actually do.

### Learn

I'm going to push you a little by pointing out untrustworthy behaviors and their consequences, so bear with me for a moment.

Chances are, if you are not happy with your money situation, then you may need to face some disappointments in yourself. Disappointments are commonly followed by self judgment, frustration, hopelessness and low self confidence.

When you fall short of your desires, you must face the reality that your actions are not getting you where you want to be. As you continue down a path of inconsistency, you

## CHAPTER 4: RE-CREATE YOUR VISION

begin to weaken the ability to rely on yourself. You become untrustworthy.

I faced my untrustworthiness when I realized that I wasn't being honest with my kids about money. I would tell them "I can't afford it" when they asked me for something I didn't want to buy for them. It became the family excuse.

I realized I just didn't <u>want</u> to spend money on what they were asking for, and I didn't have the guts to tell them. I began to break down trust each time I lied to them and myself. It would have been much more honest to come out and say, "I don't want to spend money on that" and let them be disappointed or upset. This would also have opened the door for clean and clear communication with them—what a concept!

> **Rebuilding trust is essential, and it comes from matching your words with your actions.**

Untrustworthiness also comes from making poor spending choices, being in denial, and being compulsive. When you say you will do one thing, and you do another, this breaks down the ability to rely on your word. Being trustworthy means putting your words to actions.

No one likes to admit that they are untrustworthy. It's much easier to point out others' faults and inconsistencies than it is to look at your own. This is a critical point. You must begin right now by taking an honest look at the areas in your money life where you are inconsistent, unpredictable, in denial or just not doing what you say. This may be discouraging, and you may want to give up.

*For video coaching on the secrets and their corresponding Wealth Tools, go to www.49SecretsofMoney.com*

But giving up is not an option, because it's your life! And you have visions that you must accomplish. Right now is the time to begin rebuilding self trust. Trust comes from repeating actions and seeing results. It's time to stop repeating actions that are getting you results that keep you stuck, and start taking actions you can rely on that will get you what you want.

Because you don't yet know whether your new actions will get you what you want, at first you must have faith. But, with every new action comes a new result. As you repeat each new action, you will see consistently improving results. Trust builds with consistent results. At least by trying, you can begin to trust that you have what it takes to do it!

## Act

### Build Trustworthy Actions:

List behaviors you are currently doing that are causing you disappointment, stress, or frustration.

For example, when you tell yourself day after day that you are going to stop buying that $4.50 coffee and make your coffee instead, but today, you just talked yourself out of it...AGAIN! Or maybe it's something bigger, like hiding your credit card statement from your partner because you are ashamed of the amount of purchases you've made...AGAIN.

Pick one action that you are sick of doing. Now, make a list of alternatives you could do instead. List as many as you can think of so you have lots of options. Today, if you catch yourself starting that old behavior, stop. Read your list. Try a new action.

At the end of the day, look back and see what results came from those new actions. How do you feel about yourself? If you like the results, then try them again tomorrow. (If not, try a new action.)

## Remember

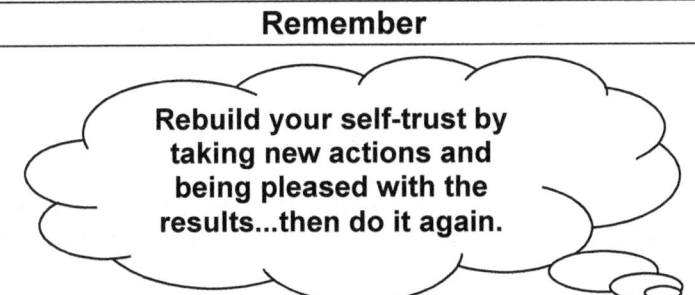

## Secret of Money #5:
## The Financial Chase

"...Life, Liberty, and the Pursuit of Happiness". Yes, it is the American Dream to pursue happiness, but pursuit is simply another word for chase. It's time to stop *chasing* happiness and start *living* it.

### Learn

Our culture sets us up for the insidious desire for more, bigger, better. It's all around us: the nicer car, the bigger house, the pervasive billboards and commercials reminding us that we need the next "thing" in order to feel better, more successful, more relaxed. This is commonly referred to as "keeping up with the Joneses." We chase a dream of financial success, yet we find ourselves running down the wrong street! Success is often defined by external comparisons rather than internal happiness. The American Dream and the Declaration of Independence have set the stage for the "pursuit of happiness" and the lasting desire for pursuing (chasing) rather than being!

The opportunity to create a life of happiness comes with a responsibility…a responsibility of personal accountability.

Is it possible to be happy and content right where you are without wanting more, bigger, better? Without excessive buying, shopping, consuming, and storing all that excess? Can you define success in ways other than financial and material success? You must know what truly makes you happy and take responsibility for creating it in your life. A lack of personal acceptance and responsibility for your current situation, no matter how bad or good it is, closes the door to your true desires.

Success can be measured by the consistent amount of diligence and discipline applied to steps taken toward worthwhile goals. To be successful, all you have to do is, 1) define your worthwhile goals, and 2) take action toward them.

Five minutes at a time, instead of pursuing the next best thing, why not pursue contentment and acceptance. Acceptance can be cultivated through understanding yourself. Really taking the time to know who you are (and who you aren't) is a powerful statement of courage and trust. Only from here can the next step be taken.

## Act

### Identify Your False Chases:

Take a few moments to think about what you are unhappy about in your life. Jot down the thoughts and regrets that come to mind.

Be honest with yourself. And dig deeply into your hidden unhappiness.

For example, I often talk to clients about their unhappiness with living paycheck to paycheck. This issue comes down to their lifestyle and/or their careers, and the discussion turns to challenging them to look at what's more important to them…the day-to-day conveniences they've embedded in their lifestyle, or the happiness they would have if they weren't living paycheck to paycheck.

Now that you've written about your discontentment and unhappiness, for each item answer these questions:

1. What are you unhappy with?

2. How are you trying to fulfill that unhappiness?

3. What would make you truly happy in this area?

After completing these questions, is there anything you need to do, say, or take action on right now? If so, GO DO IT!

## Remember

> **Find satisfaction where you are—then take small steps toward the changes you wish to see.**

---

*For video coaching on the secrets and their corresponding Wealth Tools, go to www.49SecretsofMoney.com*

# Secret of Money #6: Today **Is** Your Future

What do you want to be when you grow up? If you don't know, now is the time to figure it out. You must know where you want to go in order to get there, right? You certainly wouldn't take out a map and start driving without knowing the destination first.

So, pull over to the side of the road and plan your desired route…and discover the destination for your life!

## Learn

The actions you take today create your future. Unsure of that concept? Look back over the last 5, 10, 15 years of your life. The actions, choices, and decisions you made back then propelled your life in the direction it has taken today.

Life is a series of small actions that culminate into big accomplishments. If you want to graduate college, you don't just make the decision and "poof!" you are now a graduate! No, you have to talk to a guidance counselor, fill out paperwork, pay the fees, choose your classes, buy your books, and show up for the first day of class. It can't happen any faster than one moment, one day, one class at a time. You have to be consistent and disciplined day after day, month after month, year after year. Only then can you graduate. It all starts with the decision and the commitment to accomplish something for your future, whether that's a college degree, building an investment account, improving your golf score, or creating your ideal life.

*Create a plan to turn your VISIONS into GOAL... and your GOALS into ACTIONS.*

Seven years ago I desperately wanted to quit my job and get out of corporate America. I decided to stay, gain some additional skills, build some discipline, and strengthen my communication effectiveness. Had I left back then, I would never have found my passion for financial education, completed my credentials, earned my Masters degree, or made the connections I have with my colleagues. Today, I am clear on where I want to be in the future, so it is much easier to make day-to-day decisions because I can gauge each action on whether it will get me closer to, or farther from, where I want to be. I must take the small daily actions, 5 minutes at a time in the direction of my desired future.

And so must you.

## Act

### Design the Actions That Create Your Future:

On a blank page in your notebook draw two lines down the page, from top to bottom, dividing the page into thirds and forming three columns. Label them:

1. My life today

2. My life in ten years if I DON'T change

*For video coaching on the secrets and their corresponding Wealth Tools, go to www.49SecretsofMoney.com*

3. My life in ten years if I DO change

In the left column, describe your life now. What do you do with your time, money, relationships, etc.? Take an inventory of how you spend your days, weeks, months; and write those descriptions in the left column. In the middle column, project forward what your life might look like if you didn't make any changes. Probably looks a lot worse…right? Now in the right column, write what it would look like if you started making changes toward your dreams. Probably a lot better, right?

What daily actions could you be taking now, that will get you going in the direction you want to head? Write these down at the bottom of the page.

## Remember

If you don't change today, you won't see changes tomorrow.

# Secret of Money #7: Your Flawed Thinking

Your perspective on money is skewed. But don't worry you are not alone. All the advertisers know this, big companies know this, and the government knows this. By tying your spending to your emotions, your fantasies and your desires, it is very easy to get short term relief and forget about the long-term consequences.

## Learn

There are flaws in the way you, and everyone else, thinks about money that keeps you trapped in old ways of thinking. These unknowingly drive your dissatisfaction. I call these flaws the "CONS". The CONS drive decisions and choices based on cultural influences, not based on your desired future.

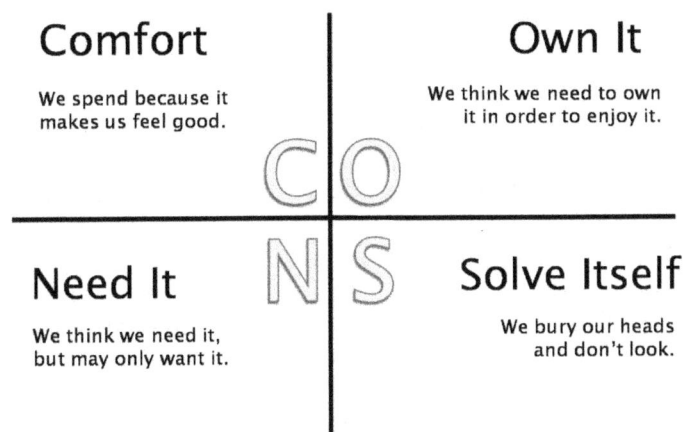

| **Comfort** | **Own It** |
| --- | --- |
| We spend because it makes us feel good. | We think we need to own it in order to enjoy it. |
| **Need It** | **Solve Itself** |
| We think we need it, but may only want it. | We bury our heads and don't look. |

Money is used to buy comfort, whether or not you actually gain the comfort you are looking for. It may provide a short term, "feel good" hit, but in the long term, comfort spending isn't nearly as satisfying as achieving maturity and emotional gratification through diligence, discernment, patience, and achievement.

Having the misconception that "owning" things is the only way to gain the experiences you are looking for is another trap. Often you can just experience it to enjoy it—without having to own it. Think about it: you don't own Disneyland, but you enjoy and remember your experiences with your family while you were there. The same thing may be true of art, vacation homes, luxury cars and so on. Do you really have to OWN them? I don't think so.

Another flawed way of thinking is that things are "needed". This is an American cultural shift of the 20$^{th}$ century…the loss of ability to discern between a "need," a "want" and an "extra."

Becoming accustomed to luxury and convenience turns wants into needs. Ten years ago, the internet and cell phones were certainly not needs; however, most people I ask today consider these necessities and they probably are. Some people consider massages, acrylic nails, tropical vacations, or loud speakers necessities, yet there are many people in the world who are happy just being able to have dinner.

For each person it's different, so without comparing yourself to someone else, you must diligently seek for yourself which items in your financial life are needs vs. wants vs. extras. We will discuss this in more detail in the H—Harness Your Expenses section (Secrets #22-28).

And the last flaw is the silly notion that financial problems will solve themselves—whether that's due to the lack of retirement funding, too much debt, or the effects of the economy on a larger scale…it seems to be much easier to ignore these problems than to deal with them.

> Another flaw is thinking you don't have CONTROL over your money. You can. And you must.

It's easier to be in denial than to face making tough changes.

It's easier to unfoundedly believe that everything will work out fine.

It's easier to take a passive way of dealing (or not dealing) with the problems. Avoidance often stems from thinking you don't have control over your

# CHAPTER 4: RE-CREATE YOUR VISION

finances (or your retirement) and that they are too confusing to deal with anyway.

These flaws lead to a feeling of hopelessness and keep you stuck on an unfulfilling course of dissatisfaction and regret. Fortunately, these flaws are easy to correct, as you will discover throughout the rest of the 49 Secrets of Money.

## Act

### Uncover Your CONS:

Exercise #1

Take a walk through your home, car, garage and so on and make a list of things you've purchased over the years, yet are truly unfulfilling, unused, or just a plain waste of money!

Are there things in your home that you've never used?

Exercise #2

Take out last month's bank statements, credit card statements and monthly bills.

Is there anything you don't want to look at?

Now circle with a red pencil everything on those statements that you purchased…yet were unfulfilling, unused, or just a plain waste of money!

*For video coaching on the secrets and their corresponding Wealth Tools, go to www.49SecretsofMoney.com*

## Remember

> Question each and every motive behind your actions.

# CHAPTER 5:
# Evaluate Where You Are

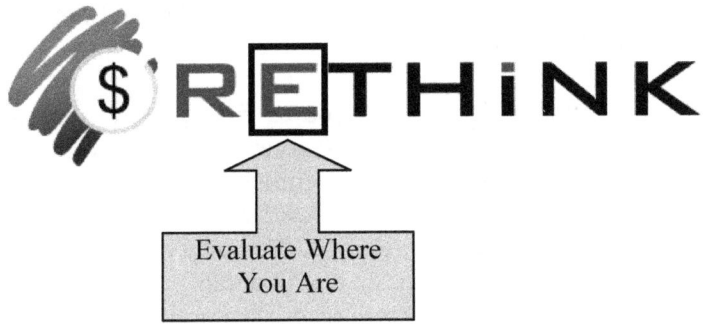

If you don't know where you want to be, and if you don't know where you are, then how will you know how to get there?

Do you have the systems in place to assess your current situation? This doesn't just mean the numbers. It also means knowing yourself...what do you do that keeps you from doing what you really want to do?

Being able to quickly and accurately assess what is happening will allow you to make adjustments quickly.

You must be able to adjust quickly in order to stay on track with your goals. If you start to get off track, which we all do, you'll want to catch it quickly so that you can make appropriate adjustments and rapidly get back on track.

---

*For video coaching on the secrets and their corresponding Wealth Tools, go to www.49SecretsofMoney.com*

If you don't monitor your finances (and yourself) consistently, you run the risk of adjusting too late.

As you continue to understand how these elements work together, you will begin to see small changes. These small changes will start appearing in your day-to-day activities such as being more aware of what's in your shopping cart, or how to talk to your kids about spending limits. Look for these small changes.

It can feel hopeless when you're first getting started. Anytime you embark on a journey that makes major changes in your life, you can go through periods of feeling disoriented or hopeless as you start to become aware of how much really needs to change. You may experience the desire to want to give up, or that you can't do it. This is normal. But don't get discouraged. You must get through this phase in order to have a new frame of reference and a new perspective on financial success.

Look back at times when you make changes in your life in the past. Whether marriage or divorce, a new career, starting school, having kids, or even in your spiritual quest. When you've gone through changes in the past, what was it like for you? Look for the stages you went through and how you managed them. You will probably go through a similar process again. Getting to know yourself better, and how you handle change, will give you a sense of confidence that will get you through this and gain satisfaction with (or maybe even elated by!) the results.

# Secret of Money #8: Evaluate Your Finances Using Your "HOMS"

You can't just look at one area of your money and expect to gain wealth and financial stability. Nor can you fix multiple areas, and leave another critical area unattended. Just like your car, you can't drive around with one flat tire thinking everything's okay because the other three tires aren't flat.

## Learn

I'm sure you've heard about budgeting. But that doesn't sound very exciting, does it? And the word "budget" itself suggests that we are working with a finite amount of resources—and this is really not the case.

No one likes to cut back or "pinch every penny". And the problem with budgeting is that most people only focus on one piece of the financial equation: where you are *spending* your money. Yet there are four core elements of *equal* importance that must be understood if you really want to see your finances improve. These four core elements are your HOMS.

HOMS is the combination and conjunction of:

> What You **H**AVE
> What You **O**WE
> What You **M**AKE
> What You **S**PEND

You will learn more about these core elements throughout the 49 Secrets of Money because they comprise four of the seven critical areas of RETHINK. Learning the individual components of net worth and cash flow (HOMS), while focusing on something interesting and meaningful, will lead to greatly increased success in realizing the financial results you want (including peace of mind!).

The keys to understanding HOMS are: <u>Your Net Worth</u> and <u>Your Cash Flow</u>.

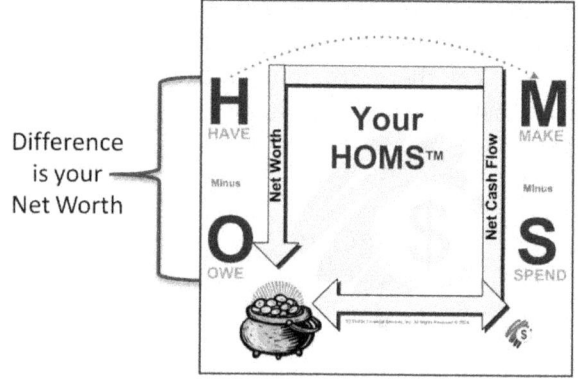

*For video coaching on the secrets and their corresponding Wealth Tools, go to www.49SecretsofMoney.com*

CHAPTER 5: EVALUATE WHERE YOU ARE **69**

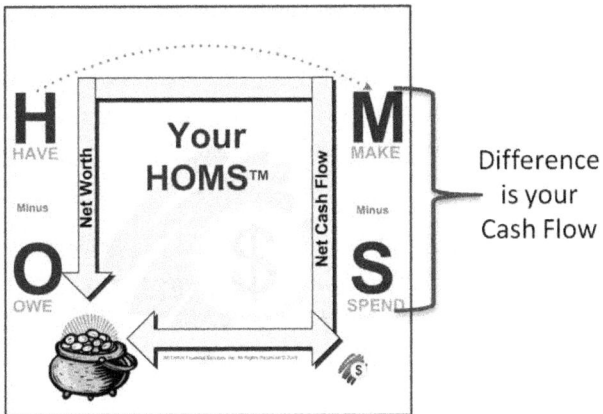

If you have positive cash flow, your net worth will increase. If you have negative cash flow, your net worth will decrease. It's that simple.

When you have positive cash flow, you have only two choices: either increase your assets or decrease your liabilities.

If your cash flow is negative, you also have only two choices: either spend (deplete) your assets or increase your debt.

You can immediately improve your net worth by making even a $1 increase in your cash flow once you've got positive cash flow. If you don't have positive cash flow yet, every step toward it is a step toward increasing your wealth.

*For video coaching on the secrets and their corresponding Wealth Tools, go to www.49SecretsofMoney.com*

For Example:

> If I spent $150 more than I made (negative cash flow), I'll have to cover that either by using my savings (decrease my assets), or I would have to borrow such as on my credit card (increase my liabilities).

OR

> If I spent $200 less than I made (positive cash flow), I could put that $200 in my savings, or I could pay down my debt.

## Act

### Improving Your Net Worth Today

When your cash flow is negative, you have the ability to improve it. It is possible. Not only is it possible, it's easy.

Start by improving it $1 at a time.

Today, make a list of 10 ways you could immediately improve your cash flow. Whether by $1 or by $1,000, list the things that will either increase your income or decrease your spending so that you can see an improvement in your cash flow right away. Small changes make a difference. Small changes add up. Small changes build the confidence needed to make big changes. Even if you can't see how saving a dollar here and there helps, it's building your awareness and creating the discipline that's going to make the biggest difference in the long run.

So, start small.

## Remember

> You can only reduce by so much. At some point, you must start increasing!

# Secret of Money #9: Your Personal Net Worth

If you want financial happiness, you must take actions to get it…today. In order to achieve what you desire, you must stop burying your head and begin to look at reality. Only then can you start doing what will bring you great success. You must change the way you think about money, and change your behaviors, one moment at a time.

## Learn

Remember, your HOMS (what you HAVE, what you OWE, what you MAKE, what you SPEND) is a depiction of your net worth and cash flow and how they tie together. Another way of portraying the "HO" side of your HOMS is creating a Personal Net Worth statement. By listing the value of everything your own, then subtracting the total of everything you owe, you can easily see what's left. This is your Net Worth:

> Total of what I HAVE
> Less
> <u>Total of what I OWE</u>
> = My Personal Net Worth

Your personal net worth is the starting point for tracking and measuring the progress and status of your financial health. If it's negative (and if it is, don't feel alone!), you'll be able to set goals to make it positive; and when it's

*For video coaching on the secrets and their corresponding Wealth Tools, go to www.49SecretsofMoney.com*

positive, you can set goals to increase your wealth and financial stability.

Using a Personal Net Worth statement on a regular basis will reinforce your discipline by giving you a clear picture of where you currently stand (no ostrich with your head in the sand allowed anymore) and help you gauge your progress. Having this clear picture will motivate you to stick to your plan.

Remember the HOMS diagram from the last Secret? Your personal net worth is what's left over after you pay off all your debts, right? Therefore, there are only three ways to increase your net worth: 1) increase what you have (your assets), 2) decrease what you owe (your liabilities), or 3) do some of both!

You will learn throughout the Secrets that managing your cash flow is the most critical element in making this happen.

## Act

## Your Personal Net Worth:

Now you're going to prepare a <u>real</u> Personal Net Worth statement, instead of one for your ideal life. Start by listing everything that you own and estimating the value of each item. Include all your bank and investment accounts, retirement accounts, homes, rental properties, recreation vehicles, jewelry, household furnishings, etc. These are your assets. Total these items to arrive at your total assets.

Now, list all of the balances that you owe, including mortgages, credit cards, student loans, personal loans, car loans, doctor bills, etc. and total these to arrive at your total liabilities. Remember to use the balance owed, NOT the monthly payments.

> Don't be afraid of the numbers. It's simple and ESSENTIAL! Not to mention, it's EMPOWERING!

Now subtract what you owe from what you have to determine your net worth.

Do you have enough?

Answering this question of "do you have enough" will be difficult to answer without knowing what you need, now <u>and</u> in the future.

## Remember

*Ask yourself, "Do I have enough?" Answer it with, "Enough for what?"*

---

*For video coaching on the secrets and their corresponding Wealth Tools, go to www.49SecretsofMoney.com*

## Secret of Money #10: Facing Reality, Taking Responsibility

Don't be afraid to really look at your situation. It may be hard to face the reality and the disappointments, but it's necessary. Feel it. And get moving!

### Learn

The hardest part of making choices about your finances is facing the reality of your situation.

It hurts to face the disappointment that you are not where you thought you would be financially. It hurts to face the losses caused by poor choices, uncontrollable events, or lack of preparation. But the only way to rebuild is to brush off your knees, give your ego a big fat hug by forgiving yourself, pull yourself up by your bootstraps, then act fast.

Find your determination. Find your drive to create or re-create a life you desire. Be creative, try a new way, become resourceful. In poor economic times, resourcefulness—the ability to find resources and to utilize them creatively—is a necessary survival skill.

Deciding to look honestly at your money means deciding to look honestly at yourself. You are the one responsible for your financial situation—like it or not. Yes, I know that there are situations out of your hands that can create financial havoc. Whether it's the economy, medical expenses, or an out-of-control ex…these and other things can devastate your finances—but they do not have to devastate your future.

> You have faults. You've made errors. That's okay. No one's judging you except YOU!

Even millionaires such as Donald Trump, Larry King, Robert Kiyosaki and many others have hit bottom, gone bankrupt or faced financial devastation at some point—and they found out how important it is to pay attention.

Pay attention by taking a close look at your role in the situation. What did you do right, and what did you do wrong? Then take from each situation these insights and apply them in the future to continually improve your outcomes.

## Act

### Take an Honest Look:

In your notebook, make a list of the financial mistakes you've made or the setbacks you've encountered. Then, next to each one, write a note about what you would do differently if it happened again.

Now, make a list of the money choices and decisions you've made that you are proud of and that have helped you. Next to each one, write a note about what you did right so that you can remember to repeat this more often.

With these lists, you now have cheat sheets to use when making financial decisions that will help strengthen your decisions and lessen your regrets.

---

*For video coaching on the secrets and their corresponding Wealth Tools, go to www.49SecretsofMoney.com*

By identifying your strengths and weaknesses, it is easier to become objective and make choices to utilize your strengths more often.

---

### Remember

> **Mistakes are your guides. Face them squarely with humility, and maybe someday with laughter and gratitude.**

# Secret of Money #11: Releasing the Past; Clearing Expectations

Holding onto expectations can be painful. Expectations often set you up for disappointment. In fact, disappointment only comes from missed expectations. Today is the day to let them go and create new ones.

## Learn

Often what holds you back from making progress are the pent up fears and pains from past experiences. In order to move forward you must stand in your pain but not wallow in it. Face it. Feel it. Honor it. This means taking an honest look at your disappointments, expectations and judgments about where you thought you should be by now.

Here you are, perhaps in your 40s, 50s, or 60s, carrying expectations that you should have thousands or even millions saved up in the bank, your house paid off and your kids' college paid for.

But the truth is, most of you have saved very little towards your retirement, owe more on your house than it's worth, and will have to borrow money to help your kids through college. Quite frankly, this feels like a raw deal, and it is certainly no fun! But it is the reality of today and you must address it for what it is.

*For video coaching on the secrets and their corresponding Wealth Tools, go to www.49SecretsofMoney.com*

Yes, it can feel sad, upsetting and uncomfortable. But it also feels real. Facing reality is much more empowering than denying it. Facing it gives you the courage and strength you need to take action.

Don't be afraid of reality. This is where great changes happen: right here in the moment of humility. Living in this moment of stark truth and embracing the reality of the situation clears the air for new thoughts, new ideas, and new opportunities to expand rapidly.

> *Okay fine. You're not happy with what you've done. Brush off your knees, and let's go!*

It may have taken years to get here.

But the speed of the past doesn't dictate the pace of the future. The speed of success can be liberating when you are completely honest with yourself, focused and motivated.

## Act

### Revealing Your Expectations:

Take the next 5-10 minutes to write about where you thought you should be financially by now.

For each of these expectations, make a note of where these expectations came from.

For example, did you learn these expectations from your parents? Or was it your peers or television that influenced you? Did you create these expectations from your own internal pressures?

Identifying the source of the expectation makes it easier to detach from unrealistic or unvalued expectations.

## Remember

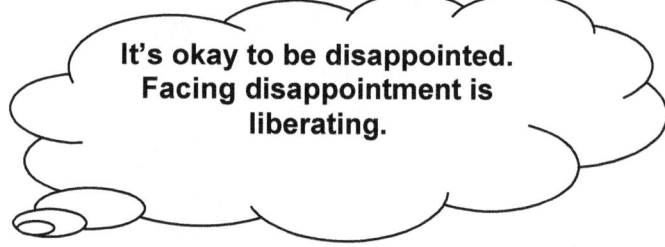

It's okay to be disappointed. Facing disappointment is liberating.

# Secret of Money #12: Behavior Assessment

Yes, you're still in the critical area of E - Evaluating Where You Are. As you can see, this is not just about the numbers. It's also about your emotions and the behaviors that got you here.

## Learn

In continuing the theme of evaluating your current situation, you must take an honest look at yourself. This includes your thoughts, choices, decisions and decision making process, behaviors, actions, patterns, habits and your beliefs that drive your unconscious choices.

You pick up these habits and beliefs both from your environment and your role models while growing up. Then as you grow and experience life, you filter your consequences through these beliefs and reinforce them—whether or not they're helping you. Whether from mom and dad, grandparents, coaches, teachers, neighbors, other influential people, or even movies and television shows, these role models impress you with their beliefs about money. For example, "money is evil", "the rich are nasty", "you must work hard for money", "wanting money means you're greedy", etc. The list could go on endlessly.

Examples of habits that are often picked up are: living paycheck to paycheck, spending on emotions, bingeing,

*For video coaching on the secrets and their corresponding Wealth Tools, go to www.49SecretsofMoney.com*

charging on credit cards, not talking about money with your partner, not properly planning ahead, etc.

You need to be able to step back from these habits by taking an assessment and making new choices.

> **Make a 'STOP-DOING' list. This forces you to admit that you're doing things that are hurting you.**

One Sunday morning, as I was feeling sick and tired of managing and juggling my bills, I realized that I happened to be really good at it. I was good at being able to manage my money so that I would pay everything but have nothing left over. In fact, I had always been good at managing money. I took pride in my ability to pay all my bills on time and maintain a good credit score with the little we had available.

While reflecting on this, I realized that's exactly how my mom is—very good at making everything work with very little. This was a great skill to have... <u>if</u> I wanted to continue being poor enough to <u>have</u> to do it!

I love my mother, and while this is not a reflection on her, I decided that day that I no longer wanted to be great at managing very little. I didn't want to just be a good money manager...I wanted to be a money *maker,* or money *grower,* or money *giver.* I wanted to break free of the skill set that was keeping me poor, gain the skills I needed to become wealthy, increase my lifestyle, and step into a new world of money. I became ready.

## Act

*For video coaching on the secrets and their corresponding Wealth Tools, go to www.49SecretsofMoney.com*

## Take an Inventory Today of Your Behaviors:

Make a list of the skills, habits, and behaviors that you often engage in. Include your thoughts, attitudes, feelings and so forth regarding money. Now look at your parents or other role models who have influenced you. Do you see any similarities?

### Remember

> Your environment got you here. Now it's up to you to get yourself where you want to be.

# Secret of Money #13: Engage Your Ideal Behaviors

Are you tired of getting beaten up by reality? I don't blame you. So, what do you want your financial life to look like? Feel like? It's taking the small baby steps that will get you there. One dollar, one decision. Each one counts.

## Learn

How do you know what behaviors you should be doing?

It depends on what you're trying to accomplish. Start with the end in mind…who are the people, the experts, the role models that you'd like to emulate?

When you identify your role models, you can begin to observe what it is you admire about them and what they've done to become an expert. If you find yourself admiring someone, but don't really understand why, take a look at what they do or represent that you value. These characteristics are clues about yourself. Jealousy, envy, or admiration are indicators that they are doing something you want to do. If you break down what exactly that is, you'll begin to see what behaviors you need to master.

For a personal example, one of my goals is to have a #1 bestselling book and a back-log of speaking engagements. I admire, and I admit I maybe even feel jealous, when I see a new book on money happiness become popular, or I see the impact of a good motivational speaker.

*For video coaching on the secrets and their corresponding Wealth Tools, go to www.49SecretsofMoney.com*

That's because I want what that author or speaker has and I am working hard towards achieving it. I am doing this because it's really important to me. Not only do I want it, but I *know* I can do it. And I know that I'd be great at it!

Without the connection between their success and my desire, there would be no admiration. We admire the people who are doing the things in life we want to do. I recognize that these people's success did not just happen by chance; it took them a lot of work, practice and stick-to-itiveness. I know I must emulate those behaviors in order to have success myself.

> **Do you admire people who are doing what you want to be doing? Maybe it's time to stop <u>wanting</u> and start <u>doing</u>.**

Therefore, I must practice writing, speaking, determination, resiliency, dedication, repetition and consistency. These are some of my ideal behaviors. If I practice these behaviors on a daily basis, followed by the right actions, I will have more confidence in attaining the outcomes I desire.

Now, I must financially prepare myself as well. My financial actions must mirror the direction I'm heading. I must change my lifestyle and match my spending and saving in ways that will get me closer to my ideals.

---

*For video coaching on the secrets and their corresponding Wealth Tools, go to www.49SecretsofMoney.com*

## Act

**Finding Your Ideal Behaviors:**

List the top 10 people you admire. What qualities do they have that you desire? Which of those qualities do you need to practice more of to achieve your goals?

What are the ideal behaviors you want to act upon with money? Who are your role models for these?

## Remember

*You are who you're around. Look around you to see who you're becoming.*

# Secret of Money #14: Put the Systems in Place

If you are disorganized with your money, then you fall right into the majority with the rest of Americans. Letting your mail pile up unopened, living paycheck to paycheck, and analyzing your financial situation by your ATM balance is the norm. But, it's also a big factor in not being able to get ahead. Taking care of your money is like taking care of your teeth…you only have to floss the ones you want to keep!

## Learn

Maybe your finances aren't where you want them to be. Or maybe they are, but you're still unhappy. The good news is, this is easy to fix with small efforts.

You can improve your net worth immediately by making small changes and applying those changes wisely.

Your Personal Net Worth increases with every $1 of improvement in your cash flow. When you increase your cash flow, you can immediately increase your assets (by increasing your savings), or you can immediately reduce your liabilities (by paying off debt)—both the increase of assets and/or the decrease of debt will increase your Personal Net Worth.

However, if you make small changes that improve your cash flow, and then use the excess you've gained by

*For video coaching on the secrets and their corresponding Wealth Tools, go to www.49SecretsofMoney.com*

spending more....you have then made no impact at all on your net worth.

> It only takes small simple steps to change your situation. But, it's essential to have consistency!

It's critically important that you put the tools in place in order to know exactly where you are financially. Preparing and reviewing monthly reports on your personal net worth and your cash flow is critical. If you don't monitor them regularly, you will not be able to assess where you are.

Balance your checkbook, get an electronic bookkeeping system for reconciling everything, type it into a spreadsheet, or just do it by hand on a yellow pad. Whatever you do, you must be able to see the numbers honestly and accurately. Don't wait until a year has gone by without looking, or you'll miss the opportunity to make those small changes that will keep you on track.

## Act

### Set Up a System:

First, create a current Personal Net Worth statement and a Cash Flow statement for last month. How easy was that? If it wasn't easy, then you don't have the right systems in place to help you. What systems, tools and software can you put into place to help you assess your finances on a monthly basis?

---

*For video coaching on the secrets and their corresponding Wealth Tools, go to www.49SecretsofMoney.com*

## Remember

*If you can't track where you are, then you'll never <u>know</u> where you are.*

# CHAPTER 6:
# Target Your Income

You can only "budget" so much...then you **must** start taking the responsibility for increasing your income.

So, why not do that with more joy, satisfaction and passion?

Being able to match your income earning capacity with your natural skills, talents and passions is essential in creating Your Optimal Life.

In order to increase your earnings without feeling like you "have to go to work", you can leverage your assets or you can leverage your earning capacity.

---

*For video coaching on the secrets and their corresponding Wealth Tools, go to www.49SecretsofMoney.com*

## CHAPTER 6: TARGET YOUR INCOME 91

Leveraging your assets starts by ensuring that you've built enough assets to produce income for you. When your assets and investments are bringing you income, you will have more time to do what you love.

Leveraging your earning capacity means utilizing your best skills, natural talents, and your passion to increase your income and the level of satisfaction in life.

Personal satisfaction comes from knowing who you are and what your unique contribution is, then putting that to action.

It's not enough to know your 'calling', or your 'purpose'.

You must act upon it.

By discovering your own uniqueness, and acting upon it daily, you will gain a sense of joy and authenticity that is much more satisfying than just wishing, or wanting. You are special. You have unique knowledge, wisdom, and skills that you have gained throughout your life.

Looking at yourself without self judgment, and with pure objective honesty, you will find those positive qualities that can make the biggest differences in the world.

I know, it's much easier and more common, to focus on what's <u>wrong</u> with you, what you <u>don't</u> have, and what's missing, rather than focusing on your <u>best</u> qualities.

But now it's time to stop that self-defeating habit, and start seeing you for who you really are. The world needs your contribution.

---

*For video coaching on the secrets and their corresponding Wealth Tools, go to www.49SecretsofMoney.com*

# Secret of Money #15:
# Your HOMS on Cash Flow

When most people think about improving their money, the first thing that comes to mind is budgeting. Budgeting is a good start, but how many of those people follow through, or more importantly, make adjustments when they go astray from the budget. It's so easy to just brush it off when you blow your budget, rather than sitting down and having a real conversation about what needs to happen. In order to take the emotions out of it, it's best to monitor all four parts of the equation, not just 'budgeting'.

## Learn

In Secret #8: Evaluate Your Financial Situation: Your HOMS, I introduced the idea of net worth and cash flow. Remember, your net worth is dependent upon managing your cash flow and using the excess wisely.

*For video coaching on the secrets and their corresponding Wealth Tools, go to www.49SecretsofMoney.com*

As a refresher, here's the HOMS diagram:

The focus in these seven Secrets is on the "What you MAKE" (your income) side of HOMS.

The point is to discover how you can make more while increasing the amount of fun, fulfillment and satisfaction you experience while you're doing it. Because so often the focus is on reducing spending, many people leave off the responsibility of maximizing earnings.

Now, I know that everyone understands that you have to earn money. But what is often missed are three key

*For video coaching on the secrets and their corresponding Wealth Tools, go to www.49SecretsofMoney.com*

> *Bringing money into your cash flow is at least as important as monitoring what goes out.*

elements: 1) taking responsibility to *increase* your earning power, 2) leveraging your earning power by using your natural skills, talents and passions, and 3) getting your assets to earn more for you so you don't have to relentlessly "work" for your income.

When you are working for less than you are worth, work in jobs where you are underutilized and under-paid, or spend too much time volunteering, what need are you fulfilling? I don't mean that sarcastically or with any judgment, just an honest question to ask yourself. It is most likely a valid need, but perhaps you can find a more appropriate way of getting that need met.

## Act

### Review Your Earnings History:

Find your most recent annual Social Security statement (usually mailed to you each year) which shows you the amount of Social Security income you will receive upon retirement. The statement also shows your earning history for each year that you have worked. If you don't have this, you can look at your tax returns or perhaps, using your best estimate, prepare a list of your annual earnings, going back as far as you can remember.

Now that you can see your earnings history, answer the following questions:

1. Are you satisfied with what you see?

# CHAPTER 6: TARGET YOUR INCOME 95

2. What patterns do you see?

3. Have your earnings been consistent?

4. Have they been consistently increasing? By how much?

5. What factors have kept them from increasing?

## Remember

> You must increase your earning capacity in order to increase your earnings.

# Secret of Money #16: Prepare Your Cash Flow Statement

I was once consulting a non-profit organization on their budget, when I noticed a line on the budget called "transfer from savings". I asked what this was, and sure enough, it was the amount of money they were planning on transferring from their savings in order to make a balanced budget. Now, this may make sense to you, as it did for the woman who responded. I understood her explanation after hearing how she did it at home, but I was shocked. There was a huge disconnect in the fact that they were <u>planning</u> on overspending, and were not even aware of the shortfall in their budget. This is a problem.

## Learn

Before we get started on leveraging your natural skills, talents and passions and discovering your Optimal Life, I need you to demonstrate your full understanding of the cash flow side of your HOMS by creating a Cash Flow Statement for yourself.

Remember…cash flow only deals with what's coming in and going out. It's important to understand what your monthly flow of cash is—whether it's positive or negative. Once you master this, you can begin to forecast your cash flow.

Learning to forecast cash flow is important for obtaining financial peace and being able to have that good night's

*For video coaching on the secrets and their corresponding Wealth Tools, go to www.49SecretsofMoney.com*

sleep you're looking for. With that, you can then prepare ahead of time for upcoming shortfalls, rather than having them jump out at you unexpectedly.

Whether you forecast weekly, monthly, annually or for your long-term future, forecasting will help you balance your income and spending to match your needs. It is the #1 key element that leads to an answer for the question, "How much is enough?" and allows you to adequately prepare. Most often this comes up prior to retirement.

But think about this...when most think of retirement, it's like there's an imaginary line in the sky where someday everything will be bliss and you'll finally be able to do what you want. But if you haven't properly forecasted the cash flow needed for retirement, how will you ever reach that "retirement line", and how will you pay for it? Will you really be able to do what you imagined when you retire?

*Use your cash flow statement to monitor your resources, track your goals, and plan for your future.*

We've all heard of the terms *debt* and *deficit*, but did you know that *deficit* represents an amount of negative cash flow? Often the term *budget deficit* is used. That means they are <u>planning</u> on not having enough income to cover the projected outflow. So, how is this difference (deficit) made up? There are only 2 choices: by either spending down reserves or by incurring more debt. That's it. Same answer every time. The estimated amount of the Federal Deficit planned for the 2010-2011 fiscal year is estimated to be over $1.6 trillion dollars! That is just for one year—

not to mention that the total outstanding debt of the federal government is already almost $13 trillion dollars!

## Act

### Your Cash Flow:

On a blank piece of paper, create a cash flow statement for yourself for last month. List all of the income that came in and everything that went out. Don't forget about the little things like parking, the afternoon snack of soda and chips, the morning coffee, or the neighbor's birthday party you purchased appetizers for.

Is your cash flow positive or negative?

Did you charge anything new on your credit cards or department store accounts?

## Remember

**On average, Americans have been spending $1.25 for every $1.00 they earn.**

*For video coaching on the secrets and their corresponding Wealth Tools, go to www.49SecretsofMoney.com*

## Secret of Money #17: Under Earning

Stop complaining about your job, your hours, your pay, your unhappiness. Your behaviors show your real intentions, so get up and do something different today. Your life is a reflection of your willingness. Your willingness will drive you to do what it takes to create the earnings you want, and it will break old habits and get new results. But you must become willing.

### Learn

Because income is a critical factor in improving your cash flow, it's important to assess whether or not you are earning at your personal capacity. One of the indicators is your level of happiness at your job and the contribution it brings to your home.

Right now, if your income has been affected by the economy, or if you've been laid off, it's a really good time to take a look at your earning potential.

*Are you feeding low self-esteem by under-earning?*

*Empower yourself by earning what you're worth.*

There are often thoughts, attitudes and beliefs about earning that keep you from earning and performing to your fullest potential. These attitudes, when based on "chasing" something, or on trying

*For video coaching on the secrets and their corresponding Wealth Tools, go to www.49SecretsofMoney.com*

to "keep up with the Joneses", often drive you into jobs that are not what you want to do. A few signs that Debtors Anonymous identifies as under earning are:

- Resenting low pay or a bad job situation, yet not asking for a raise or changing jobs;

- Believing your salary is not important, yet worrying about money constantly;

- Spending hours daydreaming but not even minutes working toward your dreams;

- Over-committing time and energy to volunteer activities;

- Overworking and spending hours to do a job more perfectly than you are getting paid to do;

- Being too fearful of failure to get any more training or attempt a new career;

- Believing no one will pay you for anything you enjoy doing.

Many times, jobs are accepted because they are simply there, or because they were offered, not because you sought them out. Very rarely do people actually take the time to seek out a specific job, identify the needed skills to be great at it, then set out to develop an education and career plan that promotes the development of these new skills and attributes.

# CHAPTER 6: TARGET YOUR INCOME  **101**

You are the one responsible for creating a prosperous life for yourself. You can take charge of your work situation by being honest with yourself. Now is the time to have unwavering willingness to honestly assess the level of satisfaction and the level of income you are earning in your current job.

## Act

### You're Grown Up…Now What?

So, what do you want to be when you grow up?

List all the jobs that would totally excite you, motivate you, and would make your heart sing! Then, list all the factors that are holding you back from being fully utilized and making more money in your current job/business.

## Remember

> It's not <u>what</u> you do—it's <u>who</u> <u>you are</u> and when you're doing it that matters.

---

*For video coaching on the secrets and their corresponding Wealth Tools, go to www.49SecretsofMoney.com*

# Secret of Money #18: Creating Earning Power

Put more of what you love into your current job, and you will be amazed at how your job may change to incorporate your enthusiasm. It is possible to do what you love right where you are. Tap into your resourcefulness and creativity to find new ways of improving your job.

## Learn

Earning power comes from leveraging your natural skills, talents and passions. Think about it. Do you ever feel underutilized at work?

Let me ask you this...do you love your job?

Whether you do or you don't, you can probably find aspects of your job that you do love. The key is to first start incorporating more of those skills into your day-to-day activities as best you can. The more you identify and define your true talents, the sooner you can build a plan to make it your full-time "job". Once you do that, it doesn't feel like a job anymore.

When I was a staff accountant at a large CPA firm, I really didn't like my job. I didn't like crunching numbers for 8-12 hours a day. One day I asked myself, "Hey, I'm an artist—what the heck am I doing here?" I had many reasons for being there, one of which was to gain discipline and to learn how Corporate America works, but I didn't want to hate my job. So, I asked myself, "How can I bring more artistic talent and creativity into my work?"

No, it wasn't by doing creative accounting! But it was by deciding to create elaborate flow charts and spreadsheets as learning tools—as tools for managing large projects and for simplifying difficult concepts. I'm an expert at that now, and I really love doing it. It brings more efficiency to my business, better communication to my clients, and is a highly valued service I can provide.

> **Bring more of your natural talents and skills into your current job. You will enjoy it more!**

I was inspired by Deborah Price, Founder of the Money Coaching Institute, and her programs to use my natural abilities with my learned skills to increase my job satisfaction and increase my income earning ability as well.

## Act

**Your Skills Inventory:**

Take a quick inventory of yourself. First, list your learned skills. These are skills you'd typically put on your resume—the skills you've gone to school for or learned on the job.

Now, list your natural talents. These are your hobbies, sports, crafts, singing, and softer skills like communication, teaching, etc.

What other abilities do you have?

## Remember

*Fun is making money at what you love doing!*

# Secret of Money #19: Leveraging Your Passion

If you're not passionate, than what are you? Finding and building that fire in your belly for something you love, something you believe in, something you care extremely about, is what makes life invigorating. If you sit on the couch and get sucked into TV or the internet every night, then stop! Get up, be alive and live your passion!

## Learn

What is passion anyway?

Passion is that feeling of excitement that comes from being able to see how your contributions make the world a better place.

When you match your talents with your passion, you can apply yourself more effectively.

For example, I am extremely passionate about teaching others how to be at peace with themselves, primarily through money, but also through self discovery, physical fitness, and self acceptance. I am passionate about these because I have valuable experience, wisdom and abilities to offer guidance in these areas.

*For video coaching on the secrets and their corresponding Wealth Tools, go to www.49SecretsofMoney.com*

> **The world is waiting to receive your unique contribution.**

I am not passionate, however, about helping the homeless, feeding the hungry, saving the rainforest or the animals—not because I don't care about all these, because I truly do care a lot about them. It's because I can't see myself making nearly as big a contribution in these areas as I can in the areas I have experience, passion and wisdom within. My efforts would be too diffused if I tried.

Sticking to the areas that best match your natural skills and abilities, along with your passion, allow you to make a larger contribution. It also allows you to do more, because you are more efficient with your time and energy. This concept applies to your job, yes, but it also applies to your community service, your relationships and your families as well.

## Act

### Passion Inventory:

Describe what passion is to you.

How do you invoke your passions? How could you integrate more of your passion into your daily activities?

How would you like to contribute more to your community? To your work? To your family?

*For video coaching on the secrets and their corresponding Wealth Tools, go to www.49SecretsofMoney.com*

## Remember

*Your unique contribution to the world is fueled by your passion.*

## Secret of Money #20: Letting Go

Now we start stepping into the harder parts of making changes...getting into action. You say you want financial peace and stability, but what are you willing to give up to get it? When the rubber hits the road, making lifestyle changes may mean letting go of some convenience, comfort and luxury. This will really be the test of your willingness.

### Learn

In order to step into realizing your true passions, talents and dreams, you will have to let go of some of the things you are currently doing.

This is a natural phenomenon; if you keep doing what you're doing you will keep getting the same results. If you want something different; you must change.

Even if you hate what you have now, it's still not easy to just "let go."

This is not a *"drop everything and change right now, for the rest of your life"* program. It's about realizing where you want to be and making each small decision and action point you in that direction. It won't take a week, a month, or even a year. In fact, it will probably take much longer. But, commitment and discipline will keep you heading in the right direction.

*For video coaching on the secrets and their corresponding Wealth Tools, go to www.49SecretsofMoney.com*

I continued to work in the CPA firm and then at a bank for another four and a half years *after* the day I decided to live my life's passion.

At first I wasn't willing to give up a lot, mostly because I trusted it wasn't the right time and I wanted to be better financially prepared. I wasn't yet willing to give up the security, the camaraderie and the efforts of trying to change social norms from within the corporate system.

> **You won't change your life in a day, but your life will change your life with daily actions.**

But, moment by moment, I became willing to give up more and more so that I could head in the right direction.

Eventually, I downsized my house, let go of eating in fancy restaurants, overseas vacations, and elegant spa treatments. I reduced and simplified my lifestyle, and I saved money. I became willing to give up security through things, when I gained the confidence in myself. This may sound like sacrifice, but when you begin to value something much greater than short term comfort, your priorities naturally begin to change.

Your idea of security must be replaced with an internal confidence, strength and faith. Security can be found in a variety of new ways…if you are willing to expand your current ideas about what security is and what it means to you.

*For video coaching on the secrets and their corresponding Wealth Tools, go to www.49SecretsofMoney.com*

## Act

**Lifestyle inventory:**

Take an inventory today of your lifestyle by answering the following questions:

1. What are you willing to give up? Why?

2. What aren't you willing to let go of? Why?

3. When do you need them? In a month, 6 months, a year?

4. What is the timeline that will work for you which will allow you to picture letting go of the items in your list you know you must let go of if you want to reach financial peace and success? Find a timeline that motivates you and use it as a mental catalyst to get you started.

## Remember

> Security isn't a bank account or a credit score. Security is self-confidence.

*For video coaching on the secrets and their corresponding Wealth Tools, go to www.49SecretsofMoney.com*

# Secret of Money #21: Skills, Passions and Making Money!

Being willing to let go of everything to do what you love is a radical thought, I know. But the key is 'willing'. Now that you have some willingness, you must discover who you are and how you can make money in an easy, simple, fulfilling way.

## Learn

So, how does this all tie together? By finding and living your Optimal Life.

Your Optimal Life is when you are living in the intercept of your best skills, your passions, and your money making abilities.

*For video coaching on the secrets and their corresponding Wealth Tools, go to www.49SecretsofMoney.com*

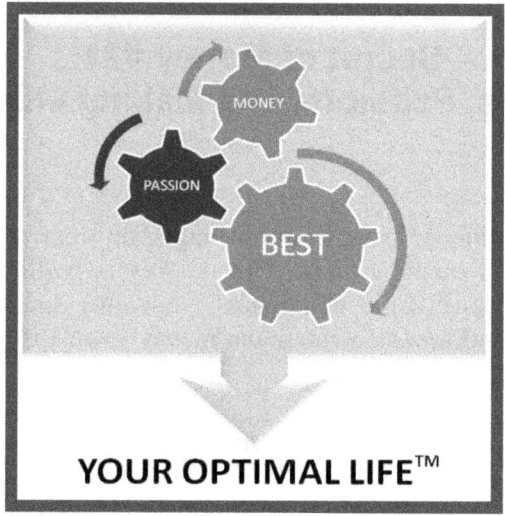

Similar to Jim Collins' hedgehog concept in "From Good to Great", discovering your Optimal Life combines 1) identifying your truly *best* skills, 2) naming your true passions, and 3) tracking them by how *you* like to make money so that you can have the most enjoyment and satisfaction in life.

Here's an example:

If, 1) your best skills are art and design, and 2) your passion is helping people express themselves, and 3) you like to make money by working directly with clients; then your Optimal Life could be a therapist; a website developer, a hair stylist, an interior decorator, or many other professions that incorporate design, expression and one-to-one clients.

*For video coaching on the secrets and their corresponding Wealth Tools, go to www.49SecretsofMoney.com*

Everyone has their own unique way of being able to make money using their passions and strengths. So, again, it's discovering yourself and utilizing the most congruent parts about you!

Without the combination of these three elements, you may be missing something. If you are living your life as a broke artist or an unhappy, yet rich stockbroker, you may be focusing on one or two (or zero) of these areas, instead of all three.

> *Liberate yourself by optimizing your life through your true passions and natural talents.*

Discovering all three areas and learning to incorporate balance amongst them is the key to living your Optimal Life.

## Act

### Finding Your Optimal Life:

Draw three circles on a blank piece of paper and label them: "Best Skills," "Passions," and "Making Money."

Fill in each circle with what is true for you. The point at which the three intercept, is where you can begin researching various careers, businesses, income earning ventures that support all three and support your Optimal Life.

---

*For video coaching on the secrets and their corresponding Wealth Tools, go to www.49SecretsofMoney.com*

## Remember

> Know yourself first, then figure out what you need—and go get it.

# CHAPTER 7:
# Harness Your Expenses

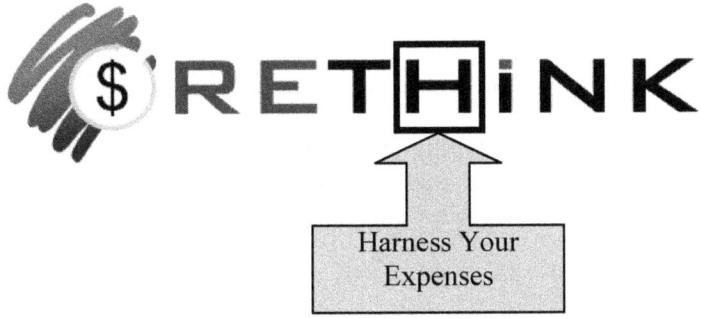

A major cultural shift over the last few decades has created the confusion between a "need" and a "want".

When material items get embedded in our lifestyle with convenience, comfort and luxury, it's easy to forget that these items are NOT necessary, but are indeed only things we **want**.

It's okay to have wants: we all do. It's okay to want luxury, comfort and convenience. But, it can be detrimental when financial resources are used solely to fulfill these wants, instead of preparing for things of more value in the future.

Often what are more valuable are the core elements that allow a good night's sleep and a sense of personal pride. Such elements are financial stability, discipline, accountability, discernment and accomplishment.

---
*For video coaching on the secrets and their corresponding Wealth Tools, go to www.49SecretsofMoney.com*

Where you use your money is a reflection of your values. By beginning to look more accurately at where your money is going, you will be able to better align your money with your values.

Several years ago, I made a list of everything I valued. Then I made a list of everything I was spending money on.

It turned out that I was completely out of alignment. What I valued most, was what I was spending the least on, and what I valued least, I was spending the most on.

I immediately knew this was a major cause of my internal discontentment, and that if I didn't change my spending habits, I would never be happy.

# Secret of Money #22: Harness Your Expenses

Living paycheck to paycheck and spending everything you earn, will not get you ahead. You may be staying afloat, you may have excellent credit, but what happens when you need to buy a new car? Then you trade your current car payment for a new car payment…and probably even a little more expensive! Why not pay for that next car with cash? It's time to stop looking at how much things are based on the monthly payment, and start thinking about how you'd pay cash for that item.

## Learn

Your cash flow has two components: what goes in and what goes out. Remember, to increase your personal net worth, you need to either increase your income, decrease your expenses, or do both.

We've just spent the last seven Secrets discussing how your income contributes to your happiness, and now we must move to your expenses. The good news is that you can only focus on improving cash flow by reducing your expenses to a point; then you must once again focus on increasing your income. As the saying goes, "you can't spend what you don't have".

The challenge is that typically when income increases, lifestyle increases as well and, therefore, expenses and outflow increase.

*For video coaching on the secrets and their corresponding Wealth Tools, go to www.49SecretsofMoney.com*

You know how that goes. You get a raise or a new job and, guess what? Now you can "afford" that new car payment, the nicer furniture, the bigger house, etc. And what happens? You're right back where you were—and where were you? Stressed and living paycheck to paycheck, wondering how you'll ever get ahead.

> **Maybe it's time to reexamine your lifestyle.**
>
> **Your spending may have increased gradually…keeping you stuck.**

Most of us don't make conscious choices to increase our expenses when we have more income. We just feel like we can spend more money when we have more. We aren't focused on clear financial goals, have difficulty making good financial decisions, and don't have a detailed plan on how to get to where we want to be.

*For video coaching on the secrets and their corresponding Wealth Tools, go to www.49SecretsofMoney.com*

CHAPTER 7: HARNESS YOUR EXPENSES **119**

Let's look at that on the HOMS diagram again:

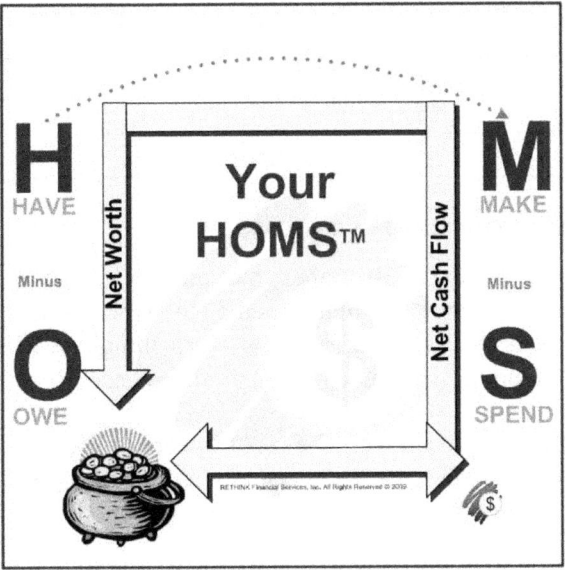

If you increase what you make and increase what you spend by the same amount, your cash flow doesn't improve. Because the cash flow side hasn't improved, there is nothing left to help build your net worth and gain financial stability for the long run.

For financial stability, you *must* improve the net worth side of your HOMS or you will always be living paycheck to paycheck.

This is a very important concept in obtaining peace regarding money and reaching your financial goals, so be sure you understand how all these elements work. If you

*For video coaching on the secrets and their corresponding Wealth Tools, go to www.49SecretsofMoney.com*

are not 100% clear on how this works, or how to make it work in your life, go back and refresh yourself on how your HOMS works. To have this make a real difference in your life, you need to be very familiar with the concepts of net worth and cash flow.

## Act

### Review Your Lifestyle Increases:

Lifestyle typically describes the quality of your living choices. This includes items such as the stores you shop at, the brands you choose, housing, furnishings, restaurants, entertainment, gyms, bodywork, clothing, etc.

While looking back over the last 10 years or so, make a list of the changes you've seen in your lifestyle. What improvements have you made? How is your life different today than back then?

## Remember

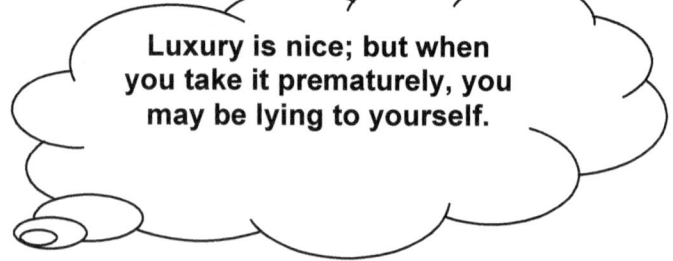

**Luxury is nice; but when you take it prematurely, you may be lying to yourself.**

## Secret of Money #23: Needs, Wants, Extras

Now it is time to drill into your spending. And there's no more difficult area to uncover than your habits and entitlements, while taking a closer look into where your money is going and why. What you think you need today may not have even existed 10 years ago. Funny, how all of a sudden we "need" it, huh?

### Learn

In today's society, there is confusion about what is a need versus a want or an extra.

The definitions used in our programs are:

1. a need is something you can't live without

2. a want is something you could give up, but don't want to because it enhances your quality of life; and,

3. an extra is something you're willing to give up in order to reach your goals.

So, why is there confusion? It seems so simple. But, when lifestyle increases, so does the sense of "need." When you own a huge house, travel often, and aren't home much, you probably "need" a housekeeper, maintenance person, alarm system, and maybe even a chef.

*For video coaching on the secrets and their corresponding Wealth Tools, go to www.49SecretsofMoney.com*

Even in a more modest lifestyle, I often hear clients say they "need" a cell phone, cable, convenience foods, gym memberships, Starbucks, etc!

But, if you compare this to the rest of the world, or to what it takes to keep a human body alive...well, you must realize these are <u>not</u> needs, but wants and luxuries.

To keep up with busy, hectic, fast-paced lives, yes, these things feel like necessities because there isn't time to prepare, relax, connect and entertain without all the electronics and devices. These are needed in order to do *more*.

> The current view of needs versus wants has become skewed over the last few decades.

Buy, why not do *less* instead?

Now, I'm not saying there is anything wrong with wanting convenience or luxury. I'm just saying that the confusion of thinking that these are *needs* is flawed. This confusion also decreases the willingness to change. It creates an attachment, and the fear of losing these conveniences is greater than looking at the reality. Hence, we stay stuck...still searching for financial peace and happiness, still unwilling to let go of what makes us feel comfortable.

## Act

### Your Needs, Wants and Extras:

Pull out the cash flow statement you prepared previously and review each of the items.

*For video coaching on the secrets and their corresponding Wealth Tools, go to www.49SecretsofMoney.com*

## CHAPTER 7: HARNESS YOUR EXPENSES 123

For each one, indicate whether it is a need, a want, or an extra (N, W, E). Remember, the definitions are:

1. a need is something you can't live without
2. a want is something you could give up, but don't want to because it enhances your quality of life; and,
3. an extra is something you're willing to give up in order to reach your goals.

Now, starting with the "extras," list any adjustments you'd like to make in your spending. For example, if you had "dining out" in both the Want category and the Extra category, you could make an adjustment like "dine out less than three times per week", or a dollar adjustment such as, "don't spend more than $12 when dining out for lunch".

**Remember**

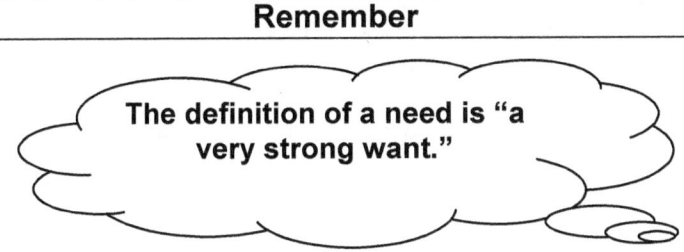

The definition of a need is "a very strong want."

# Secret of Money #24: Spending Leaks

Ah, yes. Money just leaks out, doesn't it? Where does it all go? It's like the lost sock in the dryer. You put it in, and when you go to take it out…it's gone! How does that happen?

## Learn

Ever wonder where that cash goes? While preparing your cash flow statement, you probably had a dollar amount in "cash," or "other," or "miscellaneous." Or, perhaps you just didn't remember to include the extra cash for small purchases, say, a new book at the bookstore or a gift for a friend. These things, when combined, really do add up.

These spending leaks detract from your goals and distract you from the steady focus needed to make the changes you desire.

Imagine a garden hose on full blast. The water gushes out the end, nearly flooding the area in a short period of time. Now, imagine taking a steak knife and stabbing holes all the way from the spigot to the open end. How much water do you think will be gushing out the open end now? All the pressure and flow of the water has been dispersed and is leaking in sporadic directions.

This is what happens to your money when you are not paying attention. Leaks can be small, such as a bag of chips

*For video coaching on the secrets and their corresponding Wealth Tools, go to www.49SecretsofMoney.com*

# CHAPTER 7: HARNESS YOUR EXPENSES

or a monthly magazine subscription. But they can also be big. Big leaks could be cars, boats, moving, changing jobs/careers, and overspending on vacations—all "fully justified" of course.

A leak is a distraction from getting you what you want. It is a drain on your net worth. Leaks are hard to see until you are ready to see them. Until you are sick and tired of being broke at the end of the month or not being able to save (enough) for the future, only then does the willingness to start looking honestly begin.

> **Plugging your money leaks is the simplest way to start improving your cash flow right now.**

## Act

**Your Spending Leaks:**

Imagine you are going through a typical day. List everything you might spend money on, whether large or small. Don't forget the small things like parking meters, bridge tolls, coffee, gum, lunch money for the kids (and for yourself!), newspapers, etc. If you are really ambitious, track everything you spend for seven days.

Where is your money leaking?

What do you spend money on that you *know* is a leak?

---

*For video coaching on the secrets and their corresponding Wealth Tools, go to www.49SecretsofMoney.com*

## Remember

> Focus your money in the direction **you** want it to go.

## Secret of Money #25: Decision Making

Making decisions about where to spend your money is one of the hardest things to do. How do you decide between two good things? For example, helping your kids with college vs. your retirement. Or buying life insurance vs. getting a new car. If you don't have a plan, your emotions will drive your decisions…and not always in the direction you want to go.

### Learn

What drives your decisions is often not what gets you what you truly want. Kind of like a back seat driver.

If you are feeling uncomfortable, you will often make a short-term decision to relieve the discomfort, rather than choosing an even more uncomfortable (yet crucial) decision that would bring long-term comfort and security.

Learning to say "no" to your short-term desires—and becoming willing to be uncomfortable—allows you to detach from your emotions and look more rationally at your options, choices and consequences.

Saying "no" to yourself is very powerful!

Facing what it feels like to not get what you want is also very powerful. How do you act, feel and behave when you don't get what you want?

*For video coaching on the secrets and their corresponding Wealth Tools, go to www.49SecretsofMoney.com*

I've come to realize that almost every emotion is a reaction to whether I am getting what I want or whether I'm not. Think about it. If you are excited about something, doesn't it always stem from having something you wanted, even something as small as a hug, some peace of mind, or some material item?

> **Learn how to accept NOT getting what you want.**
>
> **The urge to act out is strong…but just don't do it!**

What about the other side of that—when you're upset, discontent, mad, frustrated. Isn't it because you *didn't* get something you wanted? This is okay. There will always be times of not getting what you want. And times of getting what you want too. The point is to recognize it and remain conscious so that you have the option to react how you want to react.

Your job is to be honest with yourself. You have wants. Period. And that's okay. Once you admit that and see what's happening, then you can become willing to be okay if you don't get what you want.

The ability to discern and say "no" is financial and emotional maturity.

---

*For video coaching on the secrets and their corresponding Wealth Tools, go to www.49SecretsofMoney.com*

## Act

**How does it feel to want?**

Go into a store today and find something you would really like to have. It doesn't matter if it would cost $1.00 or $1,000.

Hold it and imagine buying it. How does it feel?

Now, say "no" to yourself. What happens? How do your feelings and thoughts change? This is not an exercise in deprivation; it is a learning experience in paying attention and staying conscious so that you can more readily recognize these feelings the next time you have them.

## Remember

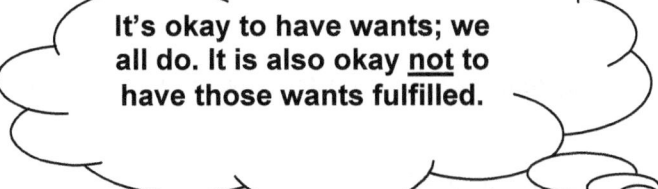

It's okay to have wants; we all do. It is also okay <u>not</u> to have those wants fulfilled.

# Secret of Money #26: Overcoming Mistakes

Do your wants and desires drive you impulsively to make choices you regret? It is so irritating, isn't it, when you just can't get that thing you want out of your head! You think about it, dream about it, research it, tell your friends about it, right? Why not just forget about it! Easier said than done, I know.

## Learn

Yes, you've made financial mistakes, let's face it. Everyone has done things and made choices that hurt them financially. Driven by wants and desires, just "having to have that newest thing", drove choices that later become regrets.

The funny thing is…those mistakes weren't mistakes at the time.

They became mistakes only in retrospect.

Think about it. At the time, if you *knew* the outcome ahead of time, would you have done it? Probably not!

You use all the information, skills, awareness and maturity available to you at that point in time to make the decisions you make. Yes, you may have been naïve, immature, unaware, uneducated, whatever; but now you know—you didn't at that time. Only hindsight is 20/20.

---

*For video coaching on the secrets and their corresponding Wealth Tools, go to www.49SecretsofMoney.com*

# Chapter 7: Harness Your Expenses

That is why it is so important to bring those mistakes up now. Laugh at them. Realize your errors and move on. Stop letting the fear of making them again hold you back today.

Use your mistakes to assess what you need now. Gain that financial maturity. Make an investment in financial education. Open your eyes to more awareness.

> **Mistakes are only mistakes in retrospect. Learn from them, and try not to repeat them.**

Set yourself on a self learning path to gain new skills so that you can protect your future from the mistakes you've made in the past.

## Act

### Financial Impulses:

Write down the last three things you purchased that were based on impulse, whether it was a vacation to the Bahamas or a magazine at the checkout line.

What prompted you to buy it? What conversation did you have with yourself before doing it?

Bring this awareness to the forefront and start watching yourself as you spend your money.

---

*For video coaching on the secrets and their corresponding Wealth Tools, go to www.49SecretsofMoney.com*

## Remember

*"Mistakes" are only mistakes in retrospect (when you realize you don't like the outcome from them).*

# CHAPTER 7: HARNESS YOUR EXPENSES

# Secret of Money #27: Cash Flow Forecasting

I've been surprised by the number of clients of all ages, and all income levels, who have a lack of understanding about cash management. Forecasting is a powerful tool that I started using on the back of an envelope in my twenties, and this tool is the simplest method of bringing a sense of control to your money right away.

## Learn

We've been talking about cash flow and its impact on your net worth. But now it's time to talk about forecasting.

Cash flow forecasting is one of the main tools you have to gain stability in your finances and peace of mind. Forecasting is projecting your anticipated income and expenses and matching them in ways that will best prepare you for a positive outcome.

When I teach forecasting, I often start with learning to forecast weekly in order to get on top of your money and gain a sense of control. This allows the novice forecaster to gain confidence in the process.

Once discipline is created and weekly forecasting becomes a habit, I shift to monthly and annual forecasting. Now you can look ahead, plan for difficult months, and be prepared financially and mentally ahead of time.

*For video coaching on the secrets and their corresponding Wealth Tools, go to www.49SecretsofMoney.com*

When I talk about long-term financial planning, I am talking about forecasting and building a plan to have the resources available to you when you need them.

In forecasting your cash flow, some people use the word "budgeting," which is a commonly used term in personal finance. I prefer cash flow forecasting because it encompasses both sides of the equation: your income *and* your expenses. Budgeting often focuses on spending, but <u>you do have a responsibility</u> to focus on the income side as well.

## Act

### Weekly Cash Flow Forecasting:

Take out a piece of paper and list all your income and expenses for the month in the left margin. Now, draw a line down and across the page to create four squares and date them for each week of the month.

> **By learning to forecast, you can immediately gain stability and peace of mind.**

Now, identify which week your income will come in and place the expected amount in its respective week. Now, place your expenses in the week they are due to be paid. Once you've listed all your income and expenses, subtract your expenses from your income for each week. Now you can see your weekly forecast and can plan accordingly to move toward positive cash flow on a weekly basis.

---

*For video coaching on the secrets and their corresponding Wealth Tools, go to www.49SecretsofMoney.com*

## Remember

*You are in control of your money. Take charge and get a handle on it!*

## Secret of Money #28: Willingness to Change

Well, you are more than half-way through the Secrets. Do you have enough willingness to change your behaviors yet? You must, or you probably would have quit many Secrets back. Willingness is one thing, and it is necessary, but another necessary aspect is ACTION! When you begin to take action, all the discomfort that you've been avoiding will start to show up. Don't back down. Stay uncomfortable, it's okay. In fact…it's probably <u>better</u> than all the stress you've been under with your current money situation.

### Learn

When reviewing cash flow, it may seem hopeless or discouraging if you're currently "upside-down" in your cash flow. If your cash flow is positive, you may still have uncertainty about the future sustainability of that cash flow. Either way, it is a good time to be real with yourself.

Ask yourself the tough questions, make tough decisions, and become willing to let go of your current thoughts and behaviors that are keeping you where you are.

If your cash flow is negative, fix it. Yeah, yeah, I know—easier said than done. But, you <u>can</u> set for yourself a solid plan with full determination to fix it as soon as possible. Then you can take direct, determined, consistent actions toward making sure it happens. You are not a lost cause.

*For video coaching on the secrets and their corresponding Wealth Tools, go to www.49SecretsofMoney.com*

## CHAPTER 7: HARNESS YOUR EXPENSES 137

But, you have to make the <u>decision</u>, make the <u>commitment</u> to yourself, and do it.

If your cash flow is positive, then you have the responsibility of planning now for the future and for keeping it safe going forward. What will happen when you retire? Are you guessing, or have you forecasted what you need and what will come in?

> **Once you make the decision to improve your money, allow your determination to drive you.**

If you feel stuck, it is probably because you've hit a place where it appears there is nothing left to do. You've made every adjustment you think is possible and are starting to feel hopeless. But I challenge you to take a closer look!

This is difficult because you must face real choices and give up things you really want.

## Act

### Give Yourself A Grade:

Revisit the personal commitment you made in Secret #1. Give yourself a grade on a scale of 1 to 10 as to how willing you are to stick to that commitment.

Now, grade yourself on a scale of 1 to 10 on how willing you are to let go of, or change, what you are doing today in order to keep that commitment.

*For video coaching on the secrets and their corresponding Wealth Tools, go to www.49SecretsofMoney.com*

## Remember

> The worst thing that could happen is that you let yourself down...again.

# CHAPTER 8:
# Integrate Your Assets

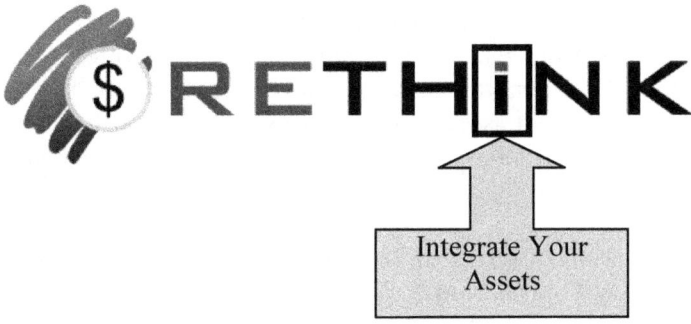

What do you own, anyway? Okay, it may be easy to list your house, your car, and maybe a rental property or two.

But what about your retirement accounts and investments?

Do you know what you actually own in them?

Besides having a gap in understanding what you own, most people also have trouble understanding the connection between what you own and why you own it.

Your assets can be classified as Safety Assets, Use Assets, or Investments. Each of your assets can be categorized in

*For video coaching on the secrets and their corresponding Wealth Tools, go to www.49SecretsofMoney.com*

one of these three ways. By categorizing them, you can better understand whether each asset is helping you or actually harming you.

Your assets should be helping to improve your cash flow now and in the future. Financial stability comes from having a plan for your assets that will cover your cash needs for the short-term, medium-term and the long-term.

When it comes to investments, it can become difficult and overwhelming. In the secrets, you'll learn the big picture about investments, so we're not going to get too technical here. Whether you have any investments at all, this is section is about assets, not just investments. You'll have a better understanding of why you need assets, what you might be missing, and what you need to do to get started.

If you want to learn more about investments, the on-line coaching program has a Wealth Tool on investments, but you can also talk with your adviser. If you have investments, I highly recommend that you learn how to have meaningful and educational conversations with your adviser. If you use an on-line service, there is often plenty of educational material available to you, as well as someone that you can contact live.

Keep asking questions until you are comfortable with the answers. Don't give up if you get intimated, you don't understand or you get overwhelmed.

Whether you have any investments or not, start reading an article or two monthly to start building your knowledge.

---

*For video coaching on the secrets and their corresponding Wealth Tools, go to www.49SecretsofMoney.com*

## Secret of Money #29: Integrate Your Assets

You've got to start somewhere, right? Start right now by understanding the assets that you own. If you have a retirement account, become willing to understand what you own. If you have no assets or investments, become willing to start accumulating right now. Then make a point to understand what types of assets you should own based on your future needs and desires.

### Learn

After managing cash flow, it's critically important that you get your assets to work for you.

Looking at your HOMS™, you've discovered how your cash flow impacts your net worth by either increasing it or decreasing it. Once you get your cash flow properly aligned so that it is producing a steady positive cash flow, then you have a choice: you either use that cash flow to increase assets or decrease liabilities. That's it. There are only 2 choices. Either increase assets or pay down debt.

*For video coaching on the secrets and their corresponding Wealth Tools, go to www.49SecretsofMoney.com*

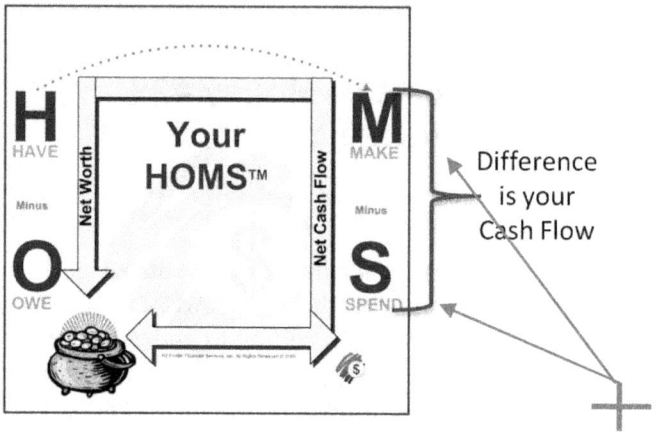

I'm not going to go into which is the better choice right now because everyone's situation is different; but I will say this—the ultimate goal would be to increase assets that produce more (passive) income and bring even more over to the cash flow side. This creates a clockwise movement through your HOMS that almost consistently increases your Net Worth!

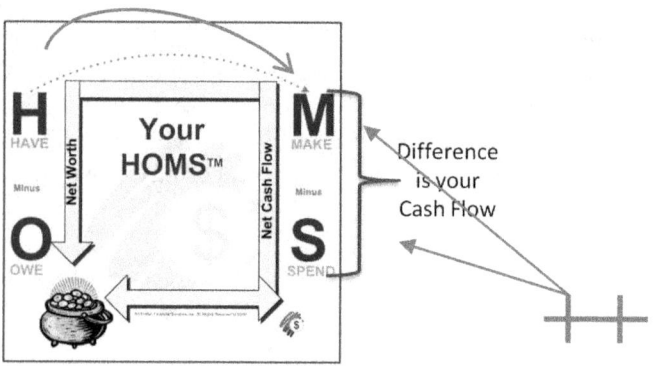

Do you see how this then begins to start growing on its own?

So, knowing where to put your positive cash flow is critical for long-term sustainability.

While you are first getting started, it is common to want to pay off debt. This is a good idea; however, it's equally important to have emergency funds in place. If you don't, you are setting yourself up for going right back into debt if something unexpected happens. So, as you are getting started, be sure to balance between saving and paying off debt.

A good rule of thumb is to keep 3-6 months of expenses in savings. Initially you may have to balance this with your other priorities, such as reducing your negative cash flow or paying off debt, but don't ignore it. At minimum, apply simultaneous strategies.

## Act

### Change in Net Worth:

Today, recalculate your personal net worth (see Secret #9) and update your cash flow.

Over the last month, was your cash flow positive or negative? By how much? What did you do with the excess if there was any?

> It's okay to build up your savings at the same time as you begin reducing your debt.

How did you fund your negative cash flow? Did you incur more debt or spend down some assets?

*For video coaching on the secrets and their corresponding Wealth Tools, go to www.49SecretsofMoney.com*

## Remember

*Get your assets working for you, so you don't have to!*

# Secret of Money #30: Definition of Assets

Okay, now it's time to get into some technical stuff. We'll keep it at a high level for now by just looking at what assets are. By looking at how your assets help you and hurt you, and why you own what you own, is important in order to get your HOMS heading in the right direction.

## Learn

In business, the International Accounting Standards Board defines assets as:

> "An asset is a resource controlled by the enterprise as a result of past events and from which future economic benefits are expected to flow to the enterprise."

This means that if it is not expected to add to the future cash flow, it's **not an asset**.

For example:

> A piece of manufacturing equipment on the books costs $10,000. It would be an asset because it will produce future revenue (as it makes the widgets for inventory). But, if that equipment becomes broken or obsolete, it will not continue to contribute to future cash flow and, therefore, must just be taken off the

books because it no longer meets the definition of an asset.

In our personal lives, this applies a little differently. To better understand your assets, categorize your assets into three groups:

- Safety Assets
- Use Assets
- Investments

Safety Assets are your cash and cash equivalent accounts that are to cover your emergencies and sustain your living if something were to happen.

Use Assets are assets that don't contribute to your cash flow and in fact actually harm it.

Investments are assets that, ideally, will bring more income to your cash flow. We'll discuss this in more detail throughout the next six Secrets.

## Act

### Your Assets:

Make a list of your assets and investments (or review your personal net worth statement), then answer the following questions.

1. Do you know what you own? (For example, do you know what stocks or funds you own in your retirement account?)

CHAPTER 8: INTEGRATE YOUR ASSETS **147**

2. Are any assets contributing or hurting your cash flow? (For example, are you holding onto real estate that's dragging you down, hoping that it will turn around some time soon?)

3. What do you own that is draining your cash flow? (For example, are you insuring multiple vehicles that you don't use?)

## Remember

> **Financial planning is having the income and assets available to cover your cash needs now and in the future.**

*For video coaching on the secrets and their corresponding Wealth Tools, go to www.49SecretsofMoney.com*

## Secret of Money #31: "Use" Assets

Ah, these are my favorite types of assets! The ones that make us look good, feel good, and leave us with empty pockets!

### Learn

Businesses use a **balance sheet** and an **income statement** to determine the health of their company.

On the individual side, we call these statements Personal Net Worth statements and Cash Flow Statements. But there is a very distinct difference on the Balance Sheet/Personal Net Worth statement between business and personal.

> If your asset costs you money instead of earning you money, then it's a Use Asset.

A business's balance sheet categorizes assets as "current" assets and "fixed" assets.

On a Personal Net Worth statement, however, individuals should categorize the assets differently: as Safety Assets, Use Assets, and Investments. The strangest category is "Use Assets."

Use Assets are assets that really aren't true assets.

*For video coaching on the secrets and their corresponding Wealth Tools, go to www.49SecretsofMoney.com*

## CHAPTER 8: INTEGRATE YOUR ASSETS 149

I think we only have this category to make us feel better, because those "assets" are usually very expensive and we want to own them. Use Assets are the things we spend money on that are not expected to bring future benefit to our cash flow. Usually these are cars, boats, RVs, etc. that will always put a strain on our cash flow as we use them, rather than improving our cash flow. They don't appreciate and they don't give us a positive cash flow; instead they tend to depreciate and we periodically spend money on them or allow them to become a cash flow "leak".

But what about your house? How does this fit? Buying a house with a mortgage can actually have a positive effect on cash flow—**ONLY when it's paid off.** That's only because you do not have to pay the mortgage or rent equivalent you would otherwise be paying if you didn't own a home free and clear. Is that what you did? Is that your plan? In 2001, according to HUD, nearly 40% of homeowners had no mortgage on their home. Then the housing boom got into full swing. In 2007 that number was 32%. What percent do you think it is now? It will be interesting to see once the 2010 census is complete!

But that's not what our recent generations have done or even have in mind to do.

Refinance—sell and buy bigger…that is the current trend!

With that current trend, there will always be a mortgage for the rest of your life and, therefore, your home will never become a benefit to your cash flow. So for most of you, owning a home will never improve your cash flow. Therefore, it should actually be categorized as a Use Asset instead of an investment.

*For video coaching on the secrets and their corresponding Wealth Tools, go to www.49SecretsofMoney.com*

## Act

**Mortgage Interest:**

If you own a house, or intend to own one, what is your plan for that home? Take a few minutes and think about it; don't just throw an answer off the top of your head. The initial answer is probably the rote answer that's expected of you. Think about it really. What will your life look like in 5, 15, 25 years, and will this house be in that picture?

Is home ownership best for you?

Today, review your loan schedule or use an online calculator to figure the amount of interest you will pay by the time you make your last payment. If you don't own a home, do this with sample numbers to understand the true cost of a mortgage. Start by picking what you think is the average price of a home in a neighborhood that you would want to live in.

On a $250,000, 30yr fixed rate 5% loan, you will pay over **$233,000** of interest. Proper planning for the right combination of down payment, monthly payments and a good strategy on paying off your mortgage early are important ingredients for responsible home ownership while going into that venture with your eyes wide open and weighing all sides of the home-buying equation.

*For video coaching on the secrets and their corresponding Wealth Tools, go to www.49SecretsofMoney.com*

## Remember

> Strive to own a home, not a mortgage.

# Secret of Money #32: Definition of Investments

Most people don't know what they own in their investment and retirement accounts. This is your money! You can learn and understand what you own, and you DO have control over your investments. Investments should help you plan for medium and long-term goals.

## Learn

In the last Secret, we learned the definition of an asset...that it must contribute to your future cash flow to be an "asset." Well, investments are intended to do just that; although, as we all know, sometimes that doesn't actually happen. But for now, instead of talking about the risks associated with investments, I want to talk about the types of investments.

Investments can be categorized into three categories:

- Interest producing

- Income producing

- Appreciation

Interest producing assets produce a steady predictable stream of income which is sometimes guaranteed, such as savings accounts, CDs, bonds, certain dividend-producing stocks (such as preferred stocks), etc. These typically

# CHAPTER 8: INTEGRATE YOUR ASSETS

protect the underlying value of the investment and have a low risk of losing the initial investment.

Income producing investments are those that may have spikes and troughs in the income and are more risky. Examples of income investments are: owning businesses, certain income-oriented stocks, and rental properties.

Appreciation investments are those you expect to go up in value and then sell at a later date to capture that value. These investments are typically real estate, art, jewelry, collectibles and certain stocks.

> *Your investments should be the tool to help you meet your future cash needs.*

Having a variety of investments and diversifying is important. Diversification reduces risk and it also allows you to match your investments according to your cash flow needs now and in the future.

## Act

### Review What You Own:

It's time to do a little investigation into what you own. First, write out the answers to the questions, then prepare for a little bit of research homework.

1. Do you own investments that you thought were for one purpose, and now that has changed?

2. Do you know what you own and why?

3. If you have a retirement account, go get the statement (open it!) and look at what you own. Do you understand it?

4. Is your original strategy still working?

Do some research online today to see what you can find out about your investments. Be curious. Ask questions such as, "what type of investments are they (stocks, mutual funds, annuities, etc.)?", "how safe or how risky are they?", etc.

One example is buying rental property for appreciation and covering the negative cash flow, thinking that it would go up in value much quicker than what you were losing on a monthly basis. The original intent was to buy it as an appreciation asset; however, this strategy didn't work, and the negative cash flow makes it act more like a Use Asset. Therefore the strategy must be reconsidered, and the realization of the error must be faced.

## Remember

Know **what** you own and **why** you own it.

# Secret of Money #33: What is "Enough"?

Retirement planning is so easy to put off, yet if you ask anyone who is already retired what they regret most, they'll probably say, "not saving earlier". It's so easy to postpone saving, but the consequences are more harmful than you think.

## Learn

Do you have enough? What a trick question! My answer is always, "Enough for what?" Sure, we can shoot for a number to hit in order to retire, but how do you know it's enough?

And besides, how did you pick that number anyway? Many times, I talk to people who say, "If I had a million dollars, I could retire—that's my number." The problem is that person may have $150,000 saved, be 52 years old, and have no plan to do anything different than what he/she has been doing. So, he/she is set up for failure, or for working forever trying to get to that one million, and still not saving enough.

Or if they have saved, as they get close to that arbitrary "$1 million" mark, they may not be properly invested or have not planned on whether that amount is the right amount for their lifestyle.

*For video coaching on the secrets and their corresponding Wealth Tools, go to www.49SecretsofMoney.com*

No one is going to fund your retirement accounts except you. The retirement system has shifted over the last few decades, and few have properly prepared for it. It used to be that you'd work for a pension and supplement that with Social Security. But, there are very little pensions left in Corporate America, and many of the previous ones have gone broke and were not properly insured. The burden has shifted to us through 401(k)s and IRAs, and we aren't saving even a fraction of enough.

In fact, on average, baby boomers have saved about 12% of what is needed for retirement.

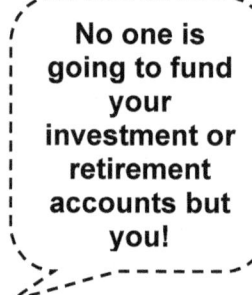

*No one is going to fund your investment or retirement accounts but you!*

"Retirement" could easily last for 30 years—that's much longer than most people's perception of 10 years or so. Most people I talk to don't even think about the reality that if they retire at 65, they could live another 30 years. It seems impossible and unrealistic to live to 95+, but how many relatives are already living that long today?

By the time that 65 year old turns 95, there will be an additional 30+ years of medical advances to increase longevity. If you're in your 40s now, that's another 50+ years of advancement. In the early 20$^{th}$ century, the average life span was 30-45. Now it is 67. That's just about double!

# CHAPTER 8: INTEGRATE YOUR ASSETS

## Act

**Do You Have Enough?**

We all have an arbitrary amount of money we think we should have at retirement. What's your "number"?

With that in mind, in your notebook write the answers to the following questions:

1. If you had that number, do you know how much you would earn each year?

2. Based on your current lifestyle, what adjustments would you have to make, if any, to live on this amount?

3. Do you have a realistic plan to reach this number?

## Remember

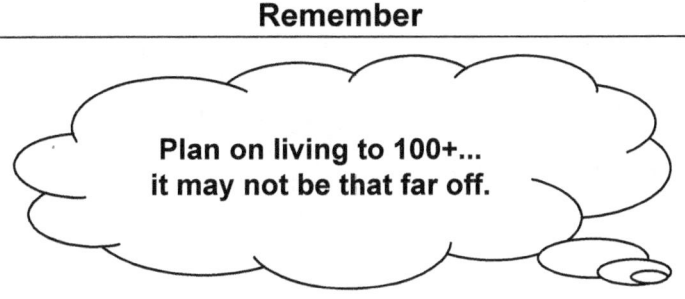

**Plan on living to 100+... it may not be that far off.**

## Secret of Money #34: Flaws of Real Estate Ownership

Real estate has been an interesting game over the last five years! Understanding the risks of real estate investing and having your financial house in order before investing is critical.

### Learn

What happened to the plan of building wealth through real estate? It all made sense—get in while you can, then flip it in a year or two and buy more, or keep your house but take out a line of credit on it to buy another.

> *It's time to look at what you can really afford, not what your broker says you qualify for.*

I went to a presentation in 2006 where they were signing people up to get insurance licenses so they could help people get the equity out of their homes and lock it into insurance and annuity contracts. "This is the 'hottest' wealth-building strategy," the speaker said, "because it captures that equity forever." His perspective was that home equity is a wasted investment because it sits there without earning anything. I wonder what he's saying today with the homes upside-down, the annuity values dropped, lost equity, plummeted income levels, and difficulty making the new house payments.

*For video coaching on the secrets and their corresponding Wealth Tools, go to www.49SecretsofMoney.com*

The other problem with riding that real estate boom was taking out equity to buy rental properties. Buying multiple properties could be a good strategy, if those properties brought in positive cash flow.

What typically happened was that cash flow was negative because so little was put down on the properties. There was an attitude that negative cash flow was okay because it would only be short-term. Once the property was sold in a year or two, there would be a huge profit that would more than compensate for the "temporary" negative cash flow needed to carry that investment property!

That all came to a crashing halt when the real estate market plunged, wages decreased, and many could no longer afford to cover that negative cash flow any more—and the options ran out.

Tech bubble, real estate bubble…what bubble is next? Stay aware that if you buy high and sell low, you will never win, and how do you know what part of the bubble you are buying into?

## Act

### Your Real Estate:

Assess your real estate rollercoaster. Whether you own(ed) real estate or not, you were probably still caught up in the hype. Think back over the last five years:

1. What were your thoughts about real estate ownership a few years ago?

2. What are they today?

*For video coaching on the secrets and their corresponding Wealth Tools, go to www.49SecretsofMoney.com*

3. What actions do you need to take now in order to correct your situation?

If you own rental properties, prepare a cash flow statement for each one. If you have any negative cash flow properties, what do you need to do to stop the bleeding? Also, determine at what point it is worth it to you to sell an "upside-down property" vs. keep it and continue to leak cash flow just to "wait out" the current market.

## Remember

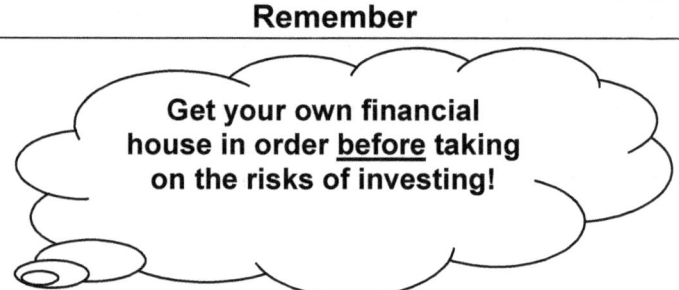

Get your own financial house in order <u>before</u> taking on the risks of investing!

*For video coaching on the secrets and their corresponding Wealth Tools, go to www.49SecretsofMoney.com*

# Secret of Money #35: Get Out of Denial!

For so many years, retirement was so far out in the future that you probably felt you had plenty of time to address it. Now, it's right around the corner, and you may be feeling a little concerned that you are not financially prepared. Facing this and what this might mean is very scary. But if you don't face it, you will still be worrying about it in ten years from now. It won't solve itself.

## Learn

It's so easy to avoid looking at areas that are hard to understand or hard to face the truth of the situation.

The fact is you probably don't have enough saved for retirement, nor do you have the wealth you want. You may be disappointed with how your real estate wealth-building or retirement planning strategy has turned out. And it probably feels like you have no control over this since "external factors" have caused this. Sound familiar?

> *Are you still holding onto regret for not saving earlier? Taking action today is the best way to overcome regret.*

---

*For video coaching on the secrets and their corresponding Wealth Tools, go to www.49SecretsofMoney.com*

In fact, you may not even open your investment account statements anymore because you don't want to look, or you don't understand what you're looking at.

A common error is thinking you don't have control over your financial situation, that the market did it to you, or the government (ah, they are easy to blame!), the economy, or the banks, etc.

But, that's not true.

You DO have control.

You have control by being willing to look honestly, to take charge of learning about your money, and start adjusting your lifestyle toward what <u>you</u> say you <u>really</u> want.

## Act

### Your Vision:

Go back and read your ten-year vision.

If you keep doing what you're doing, how is it going to get you there?

List the things you need to change now in order to gain control and take charge of your future. For example, if you want to be debt free, what are all the ways you could make that happen?

Think about things that you may not be willing to do (yet). You may want to make some big changes that you've never considered in the past. For example, you could sell your home, or downsize a car, or drastically reduce your lifestyle, if you were serious about being debt free.

### Remember

> The world sees the <u>results</u> of your actions... not your <u>intentions</u>.

# CHAPTER 9:
# Negate Your Liabilities

Are you upside-down in debt? If so, don't worry, you are not alone. America has been overspending for decades, charging on credit cards then moving into home equity. This is a factor of poor cash flow management and not having realistic expectations of the abilities to repay the debt.

Borrowing money can help you in certain circumstances and hurt you in others. Understanding the difference between debt and leverage is critical. You must know what's creating a debt problem.

Debt, or using credit on things that hurt your cash flow, is a bandage for the underlying problems of overspending and not using resources properly. Without managing the underlying issue, debt will continue to return.

## CHAPTER 9: NEGATE YOUR LIABILITIES **165**

Leverage, or using borrowed money to improve your cash flow, can actually help you. Once you've created solid financial stability, <u>then</u> you can then look to increasing your investments by using leverage.

Borrowing money can help you or hurt you. Learning how to use liabilities to your advantage, and creating a plan to pay off harmful debt, you will quickly feel a sense of confidence and control over your finances.

If you are in debt, consider how you would feel if you were debt free. Creating and working a plan toward financial freedom includes eliminating harmful debt as well as striving to increase your assets along the way.

## Secret of Money #36: Negate Your Liabilities

There are two primary definitions of the word negate. Funny that the first is "to deny the existence of", which is EXACTLY what I've been saying all along that you should NOT do! So, I want you to focus on the second definition, "to nullify, or to cause to be ineffective or invalid". Therefore, you must get rid of debt that is causing you harm, NOT deny it!

### Learn

Debt—wow, what a heavy word. But, before we go into debt vs. leverage, good debt, bad debt, etc., let's first refresh how liabilities fit into your HOMS. If you recall, the keys to increasing net worth are managing your HOMS.

## CHAPTER 9: NEGATE YOUR LIABILITIES  **167**

First taking charge of your cash flow on the right side, then deciding how to manage it on the left side, equals your personal net worth. Remember, however, if you don't have positive cash flow on the right side, then your only options are to spend down your assets or increase your liabilities to cover that shortfall in your cash flow.

Right now, so many Americans have more debt than they have assets. This creates negative personal net worth. Technically, this is insolvency. The only way to correct this is—you got it—improve your cash flow so you have more available cash, then begin paying off debt or increasing assets.

Borrowing money or restructuring debt can help you reduce payments in certain situations, and can be a good strategy. However, it is not always the best strategy to pay off debt. Sometimes building assets is best.

---

*For video coaching on the secrets and their corresponding Wealth Tools, go to www.49SecretsofMoney.com*

There is an order to using your positive cash flow to help you build wealth and be at peace. If you don't have "emergency funds" saved up, then focusing solely on paying off debt could backfire if an emergency does come up.

The goal is to continue to increase your cash flow and use the excess to strengthen your net worth. Creating a balanced strategy will help ensure long-term success.

> Remember, the goal of the secrets is to be at peace with money.
>
> Managing your debt is key.

## Act

### Your Debt:

Review all of your credit card, department store, or other debt charges over the last month. Circle the items you would <u>not</u> have purchased if you had used cash instead.

## Remember

> When it comes to interest, do you want to <u>pay</u> the interest, or <u>be paid</u> the interest?
> It's your choice.

*For video coaching on the secrets and their corresponding Wealth Tools, go to www.49SecretsofMoney.com*

# CHAPTER 9: NEGATE YOUR LIABILITIES

## Secret of Money #37: Good Debt, Bad Debt

I don't know about you, but for me whenever I get into credit card debt I feel TRAPPED. The interest, the fees, the never ending payments...whew, it's tiring and seems endless. Discipline was lost, and instant gratification was gained ever since 1959 when the first revolving credit cards were issued. The need to save for things was lost when instant credit was available instead.

### Learn

A common idea of "bad debt" immediately implies credit card debt.

This is true; however, this is not the only way to classify "bad debt." In our programs, we categorize liabilities as either debt or leverage. Bad debt equals ***debt***; good debt equals ***leverage***.

Why? Bad debt is used for two primary reasons: 1) to buy assets that hurt your cash flow, not help it, or 2) to cover negative cash flow.

For example, if you don't have enough money for those new shoes, you would have negative cash flow. Therefore, when you charge it on your card you are using credit to cover that shortfall.

*For video coaching on the secrets and their corresponding Wealth Tools, go to www.49SecretsofMoney.com*

Anything purchased on credit that will continue to hurt cash flow is debt. Good debt is called leverage because you can use borrowed money in ways that improve your cash flow. For example, using borrowed money to purchase a rental property may improve your cash flow if the rent payments you collect are higher than your costs.

> **Consumer debt depletes your net worth.**
>
> **Create a plan that you can start on today.**

Remember when we categorized your assets into safety, use and investments? Safety and use assets will not have a positive effect on your cash flow. Therefore, if you use credit to buy a "use" asset, this is debt.

Debt not only hurts your financial picture, it carries with it a lot of stress, anxiety and sense of hopelessness.

## Act

### Rethinking the Cost of Debt:

Make a list of the items that you typically charge, and for each item ask yourself these questions:

1. Why did I charge this instead of using cash or my debt card?

2. How much did it actually cost me after paying interest, fees, and other bank charges?

3. Is this something I could live without?

## Remember

> Using credit for short-term desires can bring regret later.

## Secret of Money #38: Debt vs. Leverage

Leverage is great…but it involves taking risks. You borrow money from someone in order to buy something that, hopefully, will provide you with enough earnings to cover the costs of borrowing. But…it may not. You must be able to handle the risk before taking these risks.

### Learn

So, when is borrowing money good?

It is good when it affects your cash flow positively. If you borrow money to buy assets that bring more income into your cash flow, you're on the right track.

The key is whether you make more money from the asset than it costs to borrow the money to buy it. Think about it. If you borrow $100 at 5% ($5.00 interest expense) interest and buy an asset that earns you 10% ($10 of interest income), you've just put $5 extra into your cash flow. You could do this all day and continue to grow your net worth.

So, what are the risks?

The biggest risk is trying to maintain a steady income stream that remains higher than the cost.

In order to earn higher returns, you must take on more risk.

# CHAPTER 9: NEGATE YOUR LIABILITIES

With more risk comes more volatility. If it were as easy as taking out a loan at 3% and buy CDs earning 5%, we'd all be rich and the banks would be broke. The banks make money by doing the opposite, right? They loan to you at 8% and pay you interest on your savings at about .25%. You lose money on the spread, and they make money on it.

> *The higher return you desire, the more risk you'll have to take in order to try to earn it.*

So, you have to be able to withstand risk by having your financial house in order before venturing into riskier opportunities.

## Act

**Cost of Credit:**

Make a list of the last 10 items you borrowed money to make a purchase (whether small items or large items such as a vehicle, home, etc.), then answer the following items.

1. Identify the amount borrowed and how much it costs you on an annual basis to borrow that money.

2. Note whether that item you purchased will earn any income or not.

3. Calculate the difference between the amount it costs and what it may earn.

Notice the effect on your cash flow and decide whether it is debt or leverage.

*For video coaching on the secrets and their corresponding Wealth Tools, go to www.49SecretsofMoney.com*

## Remember

> Only take on risks that you can afford to take.

# CHAPTER 9: NEGATE YOUR LIABILITIES

## Secret of Money #39:
## Consumer Debt—A Cultural Change

Somewhere along the line, we shifted to an attitude of having what we want when we want it. This entitlement attitude is tough to crack, but hopefully you are starting to see why it's so important to crack it.

### Learn

In 1959, the first revolving credit card was launched. Since that time, consumer credit has increased consistently. Step back for a moment and take a look at what has happened with our money and our attitudes, not only with the changes in credit, but with the changes in the banking system as well.

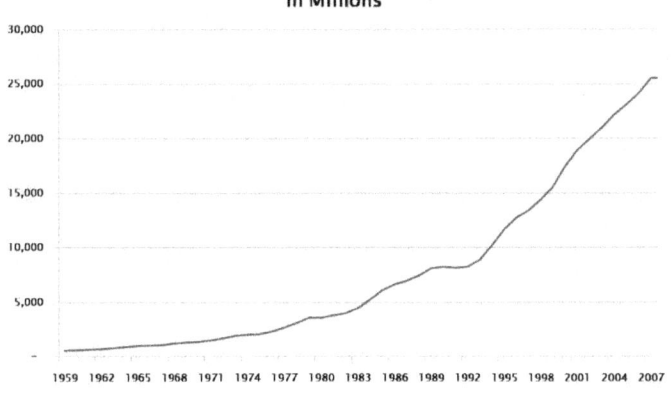

*For video coaching on the secrets and their corresponding Wealth Tools, go to www.49SecretsofMoney.com*

Imagine a time when there were no credit cards. How did items get purchased? Yes that's right. Cash was saved up to buy them, or perhaps goods or services were traded. In either case, waiting was necessary until the means were in place to get them. If you wanted to borrow money, it was a formal process of getting a loan from a bank. You didn't go get a loan for a new shirt or patio furniture like what happens today with credit cards. There was much more discernment and discipline back then.

> How quickly we forget what life was like before credit cards.

Over the decades, it has become customary to have things now and pay for them later. This is a big factor leading to not paying attention to the buildup of debt. It is much more fun to enjoy the new thing than it is to write the check for the payment after the excitement has worn off.

Another factor in the loss of attention to finances is that there is no need to balance checkbooks anymore. Many people of the elder generation, and perhaps the baby boom generation, grew up balancing checkbooks and were shocked by the idea of the Gen X's and Gen Y's going to the ATMs to look at their account balance.

At first, I advocated for balancing checkbooks, but now, with the instantaneous processing of checks, there is rarely a delay in processing; therefore, there are no "outstanding" items, and no need for balancing. The ATM balance may be exactly right.

*For video coaching on the secrets and their corresponding Wealth Tools, go to www.49SecretsofMoney.com*

## CHAPTER 9: NEGATE YOUR LIABILITIES

This, however, removed the requirement for looking at your money on a monthly basis. Knowing how much you have today is irrelevant if you don't know how to use that knowledge toward your long-term plans.

## Act

**Review Your Financials:**

Starting later today, block a time out of your schedule on a regular basis to review your financials.

Instead of looking at whether your check register is accurate (if you even use one), calculate <u>and review</u> your monthly personal net worth and your cash flow statements. Review your statements to help answer these questions:

1. Did my finances improve from last month?

2. Did I make purchases I may regret?

3. Am I on track to reach my goals this year?

## Remember

> **It's okay not to have everything you want.**

*For video coaching on the secrets and their corresponding Wealth Tools, go to www.49SecretsofMoney.com*

## Secret of Money #40:
## Investing in Education—Debt or Leverage?

Boy, how many times do I hear, "but I'm making an investment in my future!" This is true, education CAN be an investment in your future. But it can also be a big burden on your future if you're borrowing money to fund the "hobby of learning".

### Learn

We've been talking about the difference between debt and leverage—debt hurts your cash flow and leverage helps it.

So, what about student loans?

I've talked to many people...those contemplating going back to school and those who've come out of school (with tens of thousands of dollars in debt), and most think of student loans as an investment. But, let's be clear.

A loan is <u>never</u> an investment. A loan is a loan. What you use that money <u>for</u> could be the investment. An investment in yourself for education is an investment *if* you expect a higher rate of return than the cost of the education. Otherwise, it is entertainment and enrichment (a hobby), which are qualities that enhance your life, but it's not necessarily an investment in your future.

*For video coaching on the secrets and their corresponding Wealth Tools, go to www.49SecretsofMoney.com*

## CHAPTER 9: NEGATE YOUR LIABILITIES 179

To be an investment, you must intend to increase your earning potential higher than the cost of the education (including the opportunity cost of being out of the workforce). Most people don't think about this.

The expected return on investment in education can be calculated. It's a factor of the number of years in school, the cost of the school and the expected wages after graduation. The difference can be calculated to find the breakeven point and determine the amount of the investment.

> **Before going back to school, calculate how many years it will take you to break even.**

Anyway, the bottom line is this—if you can't afford school and you need to borrow the money, find out the expected return on your investment so that you will be clear on whether you are intending to go to school for entertainment or for an investment.

Whichever reason is fine; just be clear whether borrowing money for entertainment (debt) or an investment (leverage) will help you or hurt you and your financial future.

Be honest with yourself and with your kids (if you're thinking about borrowing money to help your kids). This is an area that can create defensiveness, because no one wants to be told that borrowing money to go to school may not be in their best interest.

*For video coaching on the secrets and their corresponding Wealth Tools, go to www.49SecretsofMoney.com*

## Act

**Investment or Hobby:**

If you are thinking about going to school, have already graduated, or are planning on helping your children with school, I want you to make a list of how much it will (did) cost to go to school. Include the following items:

1. Tuition

2. Books, supplies, fees, etc.

3. Travel, parking, eating out, etc.

4. Lost wages from not working while in school

5. Lost contributions to retirement accounts while not working

6. Interest on any loans/credit cards used for school or during school

Now, when you graduate, list your expected starting wage for a job with your new education.

Based on those items, ask yourself:

1. Why do I want this education?

2. Can I afford it without borrowing money?

3. How long will it take for my future wages to recoup the costs of going to school?

---

*For video coaching on the secrets and their corresponding Wealth Tools, go to www.49SecretsofMoney.com*

## Remember

> You can be a lifelong learner without sabotaging your financial strength...you just need to find out how.

## Secret of Money #41: Spending Decisions

How do you make decisions about spending? It can be really tough, especially when you have competing interests. But, you must improve your spending choices and use your newly formed financial maturity to base those decisions on your goals...not your emotions.

### Learn

Making poor spending decisions is often the cause of rising debt.

So often one goes into debt due to the lack of discernment and lack of ability to properly make spending decisions.

I'm sure you have all kinds of stories you tell yourself... and the decision process can be very painful. Guilt, shame, uncertainty, afraid of "getting in trouble", etc.

When you have conflicting desires, you have to choose between something you want over something else you want.

That is much harder than choosing between something you want and something you don't want. In fact, it actually takes away the decision when it's very clear that you <u>don't want</u> one of the factors. That is why it's easy.

For example, if you had a vase full of dead carnations and a vase full of live, vibrant roses…the decision to choose which vase to use on your dining room table would be very easy. Right? But, if one was a beautiful mixed bouquet of pink and red carnations and a variety of other colorful flowers, and the other bouquet was beautiful red, pink and yellow roses with a variety of flowers, it would be much harder to choose.

You'd have to put more thought into your decision and ask key questions such as, "what color will the table decorations be?", "how long will they last?", "do I like roses or carnations?", "do they smell?", "will they make a mess?", etc. Now you have to make a decision based on many factors.

So, why is it so hard to choose between two good things: between the kids' college and retirement savings, between the new TV and paying down a credit card, or going on vacation and going back to school? It is hard because you are forced to look into your values, and if you are not clear on your values and priorities, it's very confusing.

The clearer you've laid out your life plan and your desired legacies, the easier it is to choose. When you are unclear, you will fall victim to short-term desires, and the stories and excuses will throw you off track.

## Act

### Your Spending Stories:

Think about a time when you were challenged with a desire to buy something. Was it new clothes, power tools, a car, kids' school pictures, a waterbed, a vacation?

*For video coaching on the secrets and their corresponding Wealth Tools, go to www.49SecretsofMoney.com*

Now, write out what stories, justifications and rationalizations were happening at the time, then answer these questions:

1. What was the conflicting desire?

2. Why did you make the final decision?

3. Would you make the same choice now?

### Remember

*Decisions are much easier when you are clear on what you want.*

## Secret of Money #42: Be Patient and Consistent

To master anything, you must put in a lot of time, energy and sometimes money. You can't quit just because you're tired, bored or sick of it. This is when you must push yourself even harder. It takes time to make big changes in your life, and if you quit because it's hard or you don't like it, then you are just giving in to the same excuses that have kept you stuck all along.

### Learn

Getting into debt comes from a lack of patience and the inability to say no to your desires. Using leverage to increase your wealth is a smart, calculated decision. Leverage, as you recall, uses borrowed money to increase your cash flow.

This takes some number crunching and calculated planning to determine whether you're making a good decision or not. It is not an emotional decision, nor is it driven by a desire to have something—other than increased wealth.

If you want to be wealthier than you are, you must <u>decide</u> to be. You must face your fears and judgments about what it means to be wealthy, and get unstuck from a poverty mentality. By committing to improving your money situation, you are committing to stepping back from short-term desires and stepping into calculated decisions. You

*For video coaching on the secrets and their corresponding Wealth Tools, go to www.49SecretsofMoney.com*

must cultivate patience and discipline and learn skills to make prudent decisions.

Patience is important in two ways. One, to be able to resist the pull of the desire that is right in front of you and trust that you'll survive fine without it. And two, progress takes time. You must <u>consistently</u> apply your strategies in order to see results. If you quit too soon, you will continue to be stuck.

## Act

**Impatience:**

Make a list of five recent situations where you found yourself becoming impatient, frustrated or intolerant. Now, for each situation ask yourself these questions:

1. What aren't you getting that is creating the impatience, frustration or intolerance?

2. How important is it, really?

3. What small step could you take that will move you toward the outcome you are looking for?

## Remember

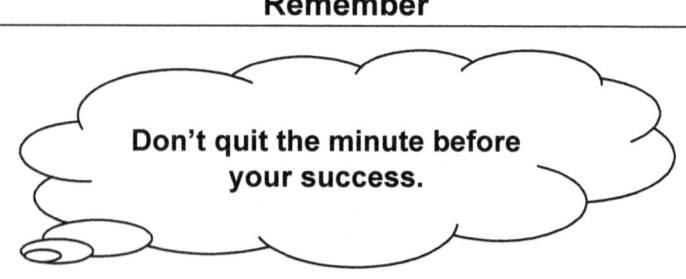

Don't quit the minute before your success.

*For video coaching on the secrets and their corresponding Wealth Tools, go to www.49SecretsofMoney.com*

# CHAPTER 10:
# Keep It All Safe!

Keep it safe from what?

YOU!

You are the biggest risk for sustaining a healthy financial future. You are the biggest risk due to your habits, emotions, behaviors, and level of financial knowledge.

Think about it...if you weren't the biggest risk, you would already be where you want to be (and probably wouldn't be reading this now), right? You would already have the personal accountability, discipline, and consistency that is probably missing right now.

"Keep it all safe" means building an accountability program, based on six-month goals, that you consistently follow through with actions that have the biggest impact on your financial life.

It means looking at all the critical areas, assessing your priorities, and creating an action plan that starts with the small steps and keeps you in the right direction.

Now that you've gained an awareness of the critical areas of money, it's time to put it all into action. By completing these remaining secrets you will create a six month financial plan based on what <u>you</u> identify is important to you.

# Secret of Money #43: Understanding Risks

Now you are heading into the final section, "Keep it All Safe". This is the most critical section, because it breeds accountability. In addition to accountability, however, you must understand potential risks to your success, both due to your actions and actions outside of your control.

## Learn

Now that you've become exposed to the key elements of building a sound financial house, you must understand the risks that could destroy it and identify ways to mitigate those risks. Risks are the events or situations that could prevent you from achieving your results. They could be within your control or outside of your control, but either way, they have the chance of severely hindering you if you are not aware of them and utilizing methods to mitigate them.

When looking at risks, look at each of the risks independently. In order to have a comprehensive perspective on your risks, go through each of the seven RETHINK areas we've been working with in the secrets and look for potential risks.

- R—Re-Create Your Future: One common risk is not being clear about whatever your vision for the future is. You'll never get there if you don't know where "there" is. Having a clear vision, and then

*For video coaching on the secrets and their corresponding Wealth Tools, go to www.49SecretsofMoney.com*

creating a solid 5-year plan will increase the likelihood of your success.

- E—Evaluate Your Finances: The risk here is <u>not</u> having a system of gathering information for your Personal Net Worth and Cash Flow on a regular, timely basis and not knowing how to use that information. If you aren't able to look at your actual numbers, you will remain ignorant and in denial.

- T—Target Your Income: If you hate your job, are unhappy or underutilized, then you risk burnout and decreased health and vitality. Your earned income can be at risk from disability, or death, while your investment income could be at risk due to improper asset allocation.

- H—Harness Your Expenses: The common risks in this area are overspending, spending on valueless items, poor decision making, and not paying attention. There are many other risks that allow your spending to get out of control.

- I—Integrate Your Assets: Your assets and investments are at risk when they lack diversification, have improper allocation, have too much volatility, become stagnant or illiquid, or are unprotected from theft or lawsuits.

- N—Negate Your Liabilities: Liabilities are at risk of being managed improperly by being too expensive, being debt (hurting your cash flow), or by being improperly leveraged.

# CHAPTER 10: KEEP IT ALL SAFE!

- K—Keep It All Safe!: This is the biggest risk of all—YOU! Your inability or unwillingness to be accountable, to take the necessary action steps and to follow through is the biggest risk to completing any of this.

## Act

**Identify Your Risks:**

Draw a large circle on a piece of paper and divide it into seven areas. Label them:

"R-E-T-H-I-N-K."

Now, list as many possible risks you can think of in each area that could hold you back or destroy what you build.

## Remember

> **You are the biggest risk to your future and your dreams.**

*For video coaching on the secrets and their corresponding Wealth Tools, go to www.49SecretsofMoney.com*

## Secret of Money #44:
## You Are the Biggest Risk

Okay, I may have to be a little direct here, but you must understand…if you don't stay with this program after the last Secret, you will revert back to what got you here in the first place. I want to see you successful, so I'm going to be direct in pointing out the biggest roadblock to your success: YOU.

### Learn

The biggest risk of your future dreams and goals, of building your financial stability, or having the life you desire …is <u>you</u>.

> How are you being a roadblock to your success?

If <u>you</u> do not follow through with the appropriate actions, if <u>you</u> do not stick to what you say you'll do, if <u>you</u> do not create accountability structures to stay focused on tasks…<u>you</u> have <u>NO</u> chance of getting where you want to be. <u>You</u> are the only thing that stands in the way.

If you want to experience the peace of mind, joy, relaxation, and fulfillment that you long for, then you have to stop doing some of the things you're doing now—and that's not easy.

*For video coaching on the secrets and their corresponding Wealth Tools, go to www.49SecretsofMoney.com*

You must be willing to give up things that provide you great comfort and familiarity. And what, or who, is going to push you when you begin to resist or start to revert back to old habits?

If you really want your financial life to be different, then set a plan for success to help you through the road bumps that will come along; otherwise, year after year you'll wonder why you're still where you are...another year gone by.

## Act

## Assessing Your Biggest Risk – <u>You</u>:

Take a few minutes and <u>really</u> think about what will keep you from taking the actions you know you need to take. In your notebook, write the answers to these questions:

1. What excuses do you think you may use in the future as to why you haven't made any changes?

2. What are you afraid you will do, or you won't do, that will keep you stuck?

3. What assistance do you need in order to face these concerns and do it anyway?

## Remember

> You have the courage not to let you get in the way...tap into it now!

# CHAPTER 10: KEEP IT ALL SAFE!

## Secret of Money #45: Protect Your HOMS

Okay, I'll give you a break. You are not the ONLY risk there is. In fact, there are many other risks that could hinder the creation of your ideal life; however, I'm not going to let you off the hook. If you don't manage this risk, you could end up right back at square one.

### Learn

There are other risks, besides yourself, that we've mentioned and need to be addressed in protecting your HOMS™ (what you HAVE, what you OWE, what you MAKE, and what you SPEND). There are three strategies for managing the risks:

1. Avoid the Risk

2. Share the Risk

3. Transfer the Risk

Looking back at the risks you've identified in Secret #43, you can map an appropriate strategy for each.

Avoiding the risk is changing the circumstances so that the risk is gone. A classic example of avoiding risk is by eliminating the object causing the risk (stop skydiving, or cut up those credit cards). You can avoid the risk of running out of resources by having a financial system that

*For video coaching on the secrets and their corresponding Wealth Tools, go to www.49SecretsofMoney.com*

includes monthly reports and forecasting so that you can manage your finances more proactively.

An example of sharing the risk is getting a partner for a business venture so that you're not taking on the full risk when starting a new business.

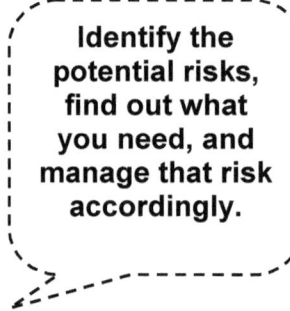
Identify the potential risks, find out what you need, and manage that risk accordingly.

Transferring the risk is putting the risk on someone else, like an insurance company by buying an insurance policy, such as your auto insurance.

So, when it comes to protecting your HOMS™, you need to identify the appropriate strategies for each risk.

That may mean obtaining disability insurance to cover the risk of losing your income due to an accident or illness, protecting your assets in trusts or a corporation, or protecting your net worth through regularly reviewing your financials.

Your goal should be to identify the risks and create a plan that reviews and monitors your exposure on a regular basis.

Once you gain the control and direction of your finances, you don't want to lose it because you weren't paying attention!

---

*For video coaching on the secrets and their corresponding Wealth Tools, go to www.49SecretsofMoney.com*

# CHAPTER 10: KEEP IT ALL SAFE!

## Act

**Managing Your Risks:**

Review the risks you identified in Secret #43 and brainstorm all the ways you could protect yourself from each one. Make a note of what you need to complete or to do in order to close that gap. You can add these to your six-month financial plan that you'll be creating in the next few secrets.

## Remember

> Protect yourself from the unwanted intrusions of life wherever possible.

## Secret of Money #46: Start with Five-Year Goals

Five years is the most I can plan for at a time. I do start with a ten-year vision, but that's too far away to set concrete plans. Five years is perfect. Once I have that in place, then I can get busy on what I need to do to get there. And so can you!

### Learn

Going back to the first seven Secrets, you identified your ideal life. Now, let's turn that life into a reality. Setting goals and targets that will get you focused is the right action needed and will get you on track. Looking now at what you want to happen in the next five years is critical. Instead of a ten-year vision, let's look at five-year goals.

Do you know the difference between a vision and a goal?

A vision is the outcome you desire, but it's big enough to be beyond your knowledge of how to get there. A vision is a combination of intuition, wisdom, dreams, desires, and reality—with a strong element of trust.

Goals are doable and measurable targets that you plan the actions toward and have a completion date.

We started with a vision in the first few secrets, and now you must turn those into goals. Goals are the steps you must take in order to reach your vision. The vision will have an outcome slightly different than what you see today because you don't know what will happen as you accomplish your goals along the way; but the vision will be the lighthouse that guides you and helps you make decisions.

> **Your vision is your lighthouse that will guide you through your daily decisions.**

After you've got your five-year goals, then you can start breaking them down into one-year and six-month goals.

## Act

### Five-Year Goals
Review your ten-year vision from the first Secrets. Now, on a blank page in your notebook list the things you want to accomplish within the next five years. To confirm that these are goals, ask yourself for each one:

1. How will I know if I have completed this goal?

2. On December 31, ____ (five years from this year), would I be able to celebrate the accomplishment of this?

3. What are the action steps I need to take to do this?

*For video coaching on the secrets and their corresponding Wealth Tools, go to www.49SecretsofMoney.com*

## Remember

To reach your vision, you must complete each short term goal first.

# Secret of Money #47:
# Create Your Six-Month Goals

With all the things you want to accomplish…and NEED to accomplish, how do you know where to start? You start by looking at what will have the biggest <u>impact</u>. You also must ensure that you don't focus only on one area and neglect other critical areas.

## Learn

Now that you have your vision and your five-year goals, here is where the rubber meets the road—identifying what you need to do over the next six months!

The key to making progress on your goals, while keeping your financial house in balance, is to set goals in multiple areas, not just one. If you focus on completing only one part, you will no doubt be missing some other very important items.

> **You will only have to complete seven goals in six months. Keep it simple.**

You've gone through the seven "RETHINK" areas, you've identified potential risks in each area, and now you must identify one thing from <u>each area</u> that will have the **biggest impact** on propelling you toward your goals…and give you satisfaction and peace of mind.

*For video coaching on the secrets and their corresponding Wealth Tools, go to www.49SecretsofMoney.com*

When you are finished with the last Secret, you will have seven goals to complete over the next six months, with the action steps to get them accomplished.

For example, if you are not clear on how to recreate your future by having a solid ten-year vision, then you must take the time to think, contemplate, discuss, and discover what you really want. Put on your six-month goal sheet to take a short retreat away from your day-to-day life and create your solid five-year plan.

## Act

### Creating Your Six-Month Goals:

Go back through each chapter and review the seven "RETHINK" areas, and all the Secrets. For each of the seven areas, identify one clear, concise, measurable, doable goal for that area that will have the biggest impact on your financial health. Your challenge is to complete each goal within six months from today.

Make sure that each goal is doable, measurable and believable. Make sure that six months from now you can look at your goal list and say "Check…completed!"

But don't make your goals simple tasks. Make them big enough to stretch you to complete them in the six-month time frame.

## Remember

> The clearer you can see the road ahead, the faster you will travel.

## Secret of Money #48: Next…Action Steps

Okay, this work has been great work. You put in over 10 minutes per day, you've heard some new concepts, you've opened your eyes to your financial house and you set your vision and goals. So what? That's right, so what? None of it matters if you don't take the next action steps.

### Learn

Here is the most important part of this whole program—your action steps.

It doesn't do any good to have a vision or set goals if you're not going to act on them. If you are not going to take actions every day toward your dreams, toward your financial health, toward creating the rich, wealthy life you desire, then what is the point of all this?

You must take actions: regular, constant, structured actions.

Often times, when I advise clients to list their action steps, they get discouraged and overwhelmed. They say, "There's too much to do, I can't do all this." And they're right, they can't.

But that is only because they listed action steps that were too big, forgetting about the "2,000 little steps" that have to happen first. This is critical to your progress. When you list

## CHAPTER 10: KEEP IT ALL SAFE! 205

your action steps, ask yourself, "Is there anything I need to do first in order to get this done?" Keep asking until you get to the very <u>next</u> thing you have to do.

But, here is another element to securing your success:

Don't do it alone!

Because you probably won't. Get someone to help you be accountable to sticking to your action steps. Use one of our RETHINK Money Coaches™, a friend, or a mentor, just as you would when you want to get in shape at the gym. Don't just go buy the membership; hire a personal trainer, get a workout buddy.

> **You only have to do the task that needs to be done today. That's all.**

Do whatever you need to do so you'll be successful.

Get your ego out of the way and make the investment in yourself.

## Act

## Create Your Action Steps:

Take out each goal from the last Secret and begin to list the <u>next</u> action steps needed in order to move you forward.

For example, if in the "R - Recreate Your Future" section you put a goal to explicitly write out your five-year goals, then what do you need to do <u>next</u>? No, it's not just "go write my goals"—it's probably something more like:

---

*For video coaching on the secrets and their corresponding Wealth Tools, go to www.49SecretsofMoney.com*

1. Ask my spouse if she/he would be willing to spend time on this.

2. Schedule a half-day trip to the beach with my spouse to talk about our future.

3. Talk to a RETHINK Money Coach™ regarding upcoming workshops or courses on how to clarify my vision.

Make sure you identify three action steps for each goal.

### Remember

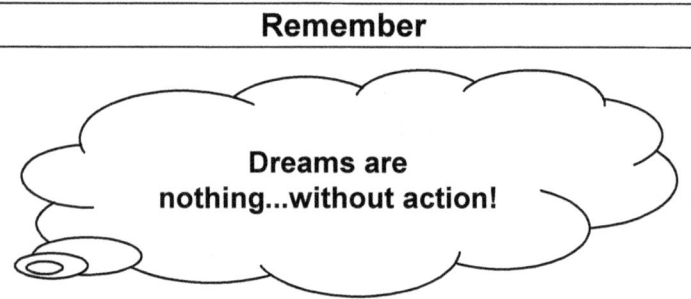

**Dreams are nothing...without action!**

*For video coaching on the secrets and their corresponding Wealth Tools, go to www.49SecretsofMoney.com*

# Secret of Money #49: Accountability

It's time for you to get serious about your life and your dreams. No one is going to do this for you. You must do it.

## Learn

Wow, you made it! You've taken this daily journey seriously and have become willing to take an honest look at what is working and what is not working in your life.

This is no small feat.

Making a commitment to a healthy, happy, satisfying future is a step ahead of most people. You've looked at your vision, your current situation, your income capacity, and your spending leaks. You've gained an understanding of your assets and liabilities and set your goals for success.

> No one is going to build you the life you desire. Only you can do it. But you must start now.

There is one last piece—accountability. What are you going to put in place to hold yourself accountable? What has always worked for me is to put my money where my mouth is! When I wanted to improve my confidence and image, I put myself through modeling school. When I want to build my physical strength, I hire personal trainers.

*For video coaching on the secrets and their corresponding Wealth Tools, go to www.49SecretsofMoney.com*

When I want to take leaps and bounds in my business, I hire a business coach. Because I want to master Karate, I hire my Sensei to train me in private sessions.

What are you willing to do? How important is your happiness? Becoming accountable will mean making changes in your lifestyle, your time management, and your priorities—changes that can be very difficult.

Are you up for the challenge of living an extraordinary life?

## Act

### Your Accountability Partner:

Make a list of 5 people who you could hire or ask to be your accountability partner. Make sure they will agree to:

1. Be nonjudgmental and objective

2. Encourage you to honestly reveal your financial goals and roadblocks

3. Call you out when you're in denial or stuck in rationalization and excuses

4. Support you and offer solutions when your world seems to be falling apart

If you are not confident that each person could do this for you, then cross them off the list.

Now, pick up the phone and call the first person on your list and ask them. Get started right away.

---

*For video coaching on the secrets and their corresponding Wealth Tools, go to www.49SecretsofMoney.com*

# CHAPTER 10: KEEP IT ALL SAFE!

You can't afford to wait!

## Remember

*If you have the ability to do it alone, you would have done it already.*

# CHAPTER 11:
# On the Road to Success

Now that you have your six-month financial plan and the awareness to get started in the right direction, it's important to identify yourself as a successful person and create the life you desire. Become a successful person by doing what successful people do:

- Successful people follow through.

- Successful people ask for help.

- Successful people stay committed.

- Successful people are relentless.

- Successful people don't let themselves get lazy.

- Successful people hang around successful people.

- Successful people master their time & energy

- Successful people stay focused!

---

*For video coaching on the secrets and their corresponding Wealth Tools, go to www.49SecretsofMoney.com*

## CHAPTER 11: ON THE ROAD TO SUCCESS

As you begin changing and becoming successful and happier, you may find it necessary to meet new friends and peers who think like you and act like you. Finding others who support you and understand where you're going will help you get there.

Old friends follow your old way of thinking and you will naturally begin to gravitate toward new friends who match your new way of thinking.

As you head down the path of living an accountable life, a life that's designed to help you create the Ideal Life you desire, it won't always be easy. In fact, if it were easy, most people would have already done it. You will encounter tough decisions, big risks and many opportunities to learn and grow. You will become an inspiration to others, while perhaps at the same time be questioning everything you're doing.

I can't tell you how many times people are intrigued by the stories I share of how I started my business, how I overcame major set-backs or how I listened and acted upon that quiet inner voice…all while I felt like I was falling apart and all my efforts were useless.

And it's funny how others are inspired by even my weakest points. Including the day I lay crying on the floor of my office in overwhelm and hopelessness. Yet while laying there in the quiet, I heard that (not-so-quiet) voice yell at me, "Get off your butt and take action right now! Nobody can, and nobody will do this for you. You and only you can fulfill this dream. No one else understands it but you. You must give them direction, provide them hope, and share your ideas!"

---

*For video coaching on the secrets and their corresponding Wealth Tools, go to www.49SecretsofMoney.com*

You may have to change friends, move, change your social habits, quit your job, or start a new business. But whatever it is, you will hit unfamiliar territory, and it will be easy to blame your discomfort and your inadequacies on others, but that's naturally just part of the process. But you're not alone. Our Money Coaches are here to help you, and I'm sure once you take these steps, you will find others on a similar path as well.

I encourage you to stay in the discomfort. Don't be afraid of it. Don't look for a place to blame, force change or fix it. There's nothing wrong or broken. It's just an incredible opportunity to astound yourself with what you can do, and find faith in the process where you never had to look before. It's your time. If it wasn't, you wouldn't be reading this today.

# ABOUT THE AUTHOR

Angie Marie Grainger, CPA /PFS, CFP®, and Certified Money Coach is the Founder of RETHINK Money Coaching, Inc. and an expert at helping people master their money by building action plans so they can transition into their new and ideal lives. Angie is a highly passionate, inspiring speaker and leader in delivering innovative, do-able, methods of teaching money concepts and thinking differently about money. Not only as an author, but her passion and enthusiasm is captured in her on-line video coaching programs as well.

A Distinguished Graduate of Sonoma State University's School of Business and Economics, and Outstanding Graduate Student from her Master's Degree in Taxation and Financial Planning at Golden Gate University, Angie blends her educational experience and her professional experience as a CPA/financial planner to anchor the

*For video coaching on the secrets and their corresponding Wealth Tools, go to www.49SecretsofMoney.com*

importance of financial accountability with the achievement of meaningful goals.

Angie is influential to other CPAs and financial advisors through her leadership with the California Society of CPAs and in building regional prosperity through financial education in her community.

www.ingramcontent.com/pod-product-compliance
Lightning Source LLC
Chambersburg PA
CBHW061258110426
42742CB00012BA/1960